THE MINDF...

Iseult White started he... ...n ... trained Apple engineers in software des... a successful technology services compan... ...j.r organisational development programmes at Fortune 100 companies and authored two successful technology books. Years of helping people deal with the fast-paced change required by new technology taught her how challenging new directions are for just about everybody. On a mission to discover how to support people in adapting to challenging life circumstances she completed a masters in psychotherapy. She now works as a psychotherapist and mindfulness teacher while continuing to support business leaders and organisations with leadership and resilience.

THE

MINDFULNESS
WORKOUT

A guide to mental fitness for teenagers
and the adults in their lives

Iseult White

VERITAS

Published 2017 by
Veritas Publications
7–8 Lower Abbey Street
Dublin 1, Ireland
publications@veritas.ie
www.veritas.ie

ISBN 978 1 84730 786 6
Copyright © Iseult White, 2017

10 9 8 7 6 5 4 3 2 1

A catalogue record for this book is available from the British Library.

Cover designed by Heather Costello, Veritas Publications
Typeset by Barbara Croatto, Veritas Publications
Printed in the Republic of Ireland by KC Print, Kerry

Veritas books are printed on paper made from the wood pulp of managed forests. For every tree felled, at least one tree is planted, thereby renewing natural resources.

For Lilly, Mirinn, Kia, Béla, Zoé and Margaux
with all my love

contents

Preface

This book integrates a number of strands of my life: my personal mindfulness practice; the lessons I have learned as a stepmother and mother of four teenagers; and my work as a mindfulness teacher and an integrative psychotherapist.

My mindfulness practice started when I first learned to meditate at the age of fourteen. As a teenager, I was at best an intermittent meditator, but as an adult I always found my way back to mindfulness in times of distress and eventually it became woven into my daily life. For me, mindfulness is an early morning walk in the park with my dogs, the birds singing, the cherry blossoms drifting, the morning light shimmering on the pond, and the chat and banter of park life. It is the space I sometimes manage to achieve when my teenagers give me that scornful look, the one that makes my blood boil, and it is the self-forgiveness for the times that I lose it and go on an unmerciful rant. Mindfulness is the spaciousness that cushions me, no matter how dark and troubling life is at times. It is my sense of the continuity of creation and the rise and the fall of the ten thousand things. It is summed up in my personal mantra, 'The sun still shines and the trees keep growing'.

When I became, almost instantaneously, a mother of four children – stepmother of two teenagers and mother of two infants – my parenting skills were challenged in the extreme. Over time I learned to be a 'stepped-back' mother rather than a stepmother. As such, I only intervened if I felt someone's physical safety was at risk or if I felt someone wasn't being respectful; just about everything else I left to my stepchildren to figure out. At the same time, I cared deeply about what was going on in their lives and I was always available when they asked for assistance or support. As my two younger children reached adolescence I discovered that the same stepped-back approach worked well for them, and we have muddled along together very nicely. I bring that stepped-back approach into my work with teenagers too.

Mindfulness is a core part of my work. I teach mindfulness for corporate wellness and leadership programmes and I integrate mindfulness into my practice as a psychotherapist. My approach to mindfulness is all-embracing and I don't subscribe to any one set of teachings. I am influenced by insight dialogue, acceptance and commitment therapy, mindfulness-based cognitive therapy, dialectical behavioural therapy, and I love the clarity of Eugene Gendlin and Ann Weiser Cornell's work on focusing, which I understand to be a form of embodied mindfulness.

I have tried to write this book in the same conversational style that I use with my clients. My hope is that it will give adults a sense of how to incorporate mindfulness into their work with teenagers, while at the same time remaining accessible to teenagers who are interested in learning about mindfulness. Background information is, for the most part, addressed to adults, parents, teachers and others who work with teenagers; however, because they are intended for use by teenagers, the exercises and mindfulness practices are addressed directly to teenagers.

I have only one word of caution: if you plan to use these exercises with teenagers, make sure that you have fully explored them for yourself first. Mindfulness is one of those things that can only be learned experientially; a book is just a jumping-off point.

Finally, I would like to thank all the young people who have graced my life with their presence. I treasure my time sitting with you and feel honoured that you share your troubles and your dreams with me. Each and every one of you teaches me something new and I hope you will accept this book as my way of paying those teachings forward.

Mindfulness Exercises

one

Start Where You Are

Teenagers have always gotten a bad rap. Back in the sixteenth century Shakespeare reckoned that between the ages of sixteen and twenty-three 'there is nothing in the between but getting wenches with child, wronging the ancientry, stealing, fighting'.

Many people believe that the teenage years are destined to be stressful for everybody involved. But in my experience, as a psychotherapist who works with teenagers and as a mother who has raised four teenagers, there are ways of dealing with the stresses, so that everybody involved can enjoy these important, creative and fun years.

If you are a parent, a teacher, a guidance counsellor, a psychotherapist, or a sports coach who works with teenagers, my hope is that the ideas in this book will help you find ways of enjoying your time with teenagers, and supporting them through the inevitable challenges they will face.

Similarly, if you are a teenager, I hope this book will help you better understand your feelings, thoughts and behaviours, and encourage you to find creative ways of dealing with the stresses in your life.

Teenagers and Stress

The teenage years are among the most stressful in life. Teenagers have to contend with a massive restructuring process in their brains, and it is this, more than hormonal changes, that is linked with the familiar and dramatic variations in mood that teenagers experience. Human brains have two major developmental periods: from birth to two, and then from the onset of puberty until twenty-five. In this second and longer developmental period, the brain goes through a major remodelling, a remodelling so huge it is like tearing down a house and rebuilding it from the ground up.

In any building project there are periods of great chaos, where nothing is connected, and everything looks messy. Similarly, there is chaos in the teenage brain, leading to emotional turmoil for everybody involved. From one minute to the next teenagers' moods may change drastically, swinging from heights of euphoria and ecstasy to the depths of darkness, despair and even destruction.

As adults, we forget how deeply teenagers feel, and we often dismiss their emotional states as overblown drama. For the teenagers, their experience and feelings are very real, and these feelings are further complicated by the fact that their concept of time has not fully developed. When they feel troubled they can end up believing that they are going to be stuck in a vortex of distress forever. During the latter part of the remodelling process, the teenage brain gains a more realistic sense of time and develops the neural networks for managing emotional upheaval. In psychology we call this capacity 'emotion regulation'.

Emotion regulation is the foundation of well-being and resilience, academic and vocational achievement, and life-enhancing relationships. Put simply, emotion regulation means the ability to handle distress without withdrawing socially, worrying excessively, or acting out angrily. Teenagers with a low tolerance for distress are more likely to develop mental health problems such as anxiety, depression, eating disorders, engage in harmful risk-taking, or use substances to manage their mood.

As if this remodelling project was not enough to contend with, teenagers face constant pressure in their lives. They are trying to separate from their parents and develop their own identity and views; this frequently leads to tension between teenagers and their parents. At the same time, they are trying desperately to fit in and be liked and accepted by their peers. They can end up feeling isolated in all areas of their lives. On top of these relational problems, they are under constant pressure to perform, academically, socially, and in sports. At every turn they find somebody somewhere is measuring their performance, whether it is their parents, their teachers, their peers or themselves.

As a psychotherapist, I work with teenagers and young adults who are feeling overwhelmed by life. By the time they arrive in my office they have been feeling distressed for a long time, counted in years rather than months. Teenagers are good at hiding their pain so it can take the adults in their lives a long time to notice. By the time they do, the 'problem' has reached a level of distress that makes it diagnosable as a mental health issue; such as eating disorder, substance abuse, depression, gaming addiction, anxiety, suicidal thoughts, or dealing with the consequences of bullying. Twenty per cent of teenagers experience a mental health problem in any given year (WHO, 2003), yet seventy per cent do not get appropriate interventions at a sufficiently early age (Children's Society, 2008).

No matter what packaging a teenager's distress comes in, the same core issues come up again and again. They cannot regulate their emotions and lack constructive ways of managing their distress. When I am working with teenagers I focus on helping them put emotion-regulation skills in place and help them create healthy and joyful connections with their peers and family. When teenagers feel less overwhelmed it creates space for their natural creativity to enter the picture, and they find innovative ways to make their lives better. I draw from the latest research in neuroscience, and use a variety of approaches based on mindfulness, combined with positive psychology, to help them find ways to create this space. Then I trust their innate capacity to grow and develop. Over the years, I have seen deeply distressed teenagers make huge changes in their lives and grow up to be thoughtful, happy, creative adults.

This book is about equipping teenagers and the adults they know with practical strategies to develop the capacity for emotion regulation long before a diagnosable mental health problem emerges. Consider these strategies an emotional and psychological form of exercise. They build mental fitness and emotional resilience, just as exercise builds cardio fitness and muscle strength.

Engaging Teenagers

While working with teenagers I have noticed certain things are important to them.

They like evidence

Teenagers are a sceptical bunch, and they are programmed to dismiss much of what adults tell them. It is easier to engage teenagers when you can provide evidence that the approaches you are suggesting have a firm foundation. That is why the ideas in this book are backed up by research that demonstrates their effectiveness.

They want to understand the rationale

Teenagers want to understand why something is useful. It is important to be able to explain the rationale in concrete specifics rather than abstract concepts. Chapter two describes what life is like for a teenage brain and explains why mindfulness makes things better.

They like things that are easy to learn and quick to apply
Teenagers are busy people. They live in a fast-paced world within an ever-changing landscape. They are under a lot of pressure in school and they have a lot of socialising to fit in. If you want them to adopt new approaches to dealing with life, those approaches have to be easy to learn and apply. The exercises in this book are simple and practical, and can be used throughout the day.

They are motivated by reward
If you are trying to motivate a teenager, always choose the carrot instead of the stick. Teenagers work better when they understand the possible rewards of doing something. Lecturing them about negative consequences is not helpful. Showing how something helps them works much better. In the next section I explain the benefits of mindfulness, and throughout the book I give practical examples, drawn from my work with teenagers, of how and where a teenager used these approaches in their own life.

They like real-life examples
Teenagers like concrete examples drawn from real life. They like to hear about other teenagers, and about people they know through the media, such as sports personalities or celebrities. Wherever possible, I provide vignettes drawn from my work, though, due to client confidentiality, none of the cases represent real clients or describe actual client material.

Why Mindfulness?

Mindfulness is a hot topic at the moment. There are thousands of research studies examining the benefits of mindfulness. Virtually every major technology company – Google, Twitter, Facebook and LinkedIn – offers mindfulness training to its employees. Organisations as diverse as banks, prisons, schools and the military have rolled out mindfulness programmes. Studies in schools have found that regular mindfulness practice improves mental health and well-being, mood, self-esteem, emotional regulation, and boosts positive behaviour and academic learning for both students and teachers.

When I talk to teenagers, I find that most of them believe mindfulness is for the fairies, the do-gooders, or something adults do that would never apply to their lives. They imagine I am going to ask them to sit cross-legged on a cushion and chant for hours on end. In order to engage their attention, the first thing I do is explain some of the benefits of mindfulness, benefits that have been backed up by scientific research.

Mindfulness is Good for Concentration
Mindfulness helps you direct your attention, so that you are less easily distracted. By consistently bringing your attention to the present, just noticing what is happening right now, rather than being caught up in thoughts about the past or future, or distracted by external stimuli in the environment, mindfulness trains your attention and increases your concentration. According to a study published in *Psychological Science*, mindfulness can increase your grades by improving your focus so you can manage your mind when it wanders (Baird, 2012). Students in the study saw a 16 per cent boost in just two weeks of mindfulness practice, and nobody had to sit cross-legged on a cushion!

Mindfulness Helps You Perform Better at an Elite Level
Imagine you are getting ready for the most important shot in your sporting career. You are only one point ahead of the competition, and if you don't make this shot, the match is lost. Your heart is racing and your body is tense. To be

successful you need to focus on the shot, taking into account the important things that are going on in your environment, perhaps the wind speed, or the position of your opponents. Mindfulness helps you focus on the present moment and gives you the mental strength to handle the intense pressure of the moment. Many top athletes have talked about how mindfulness has helped them in their sport. These include NBA players Kobe Bryant, Michael Jordan, LeBron James; tennis world number one Novak Djokovic; rugby players Rob Kearney and Jonny Wilkinson; US Volleyball Olympians Kerri Walsh and April Ross; and members of the USA women's soccer team.

Mindfulness Improves Your Physical Health
Mindfulness can even strengthen the immune system and reduce the impact of stress on physical health. One study showed that after just five days of mindfulness training students recovered faster after a stressful event and their immune system function improved. They reported feeling less anxiety, depression and anger. Indeed, the parts of our brain that are engaged by mindfulness – the prefrontal cortex, the right anterior insulate and the right hippocampus – act as our immune system's command centre. When activity in these parts of the brain increases through mindfulness, the immune system functions more effectively. Mindfulness also reduces levels of inflammation and it increases the immune system's helper cells, helping fight infection. This is good for physical health because high levels of inflammation are correlated with a decrease in immune function and the development of chronic diseases like cardiovascular disease, type 2 diabetes and autoimmune conditions.

Mindfulness reduces anxiety and depression

There is consistent evidence that mindfulness reduces symptoms of anxiety and depression. Often people with anxiety or depression are consumed by powerfully distracting thoughts. For instance, thinking 'That was a stupid thing I said ... now they are all going to hate me ... I am never going to have any friends'. But it doesn't stop there; those thoughts are repeated on a loop, increasing feelings of anxiety and depression. In psychology this is called rumination. Mindfulness helps you challenge negative thoughts and feelings, thus reducing levels of anxiety and depression.

Moving from autopilot to mindfulness

We spend a lot of time on autopilot, a constant stream of thoughts running through our minds, doing familiar tasks without thinking about them. This is useful because a lot of the things we do in life are quite dull and repetitive, and being able to do them on autopilot frees us up to think about other things. Unfortunately, we often spend a lot of time on autopilot when we are supposed to be focusing on something important, like listening in class or studying for exams.

Have you ever sat down at your desk to make revision notes? You gather your books and your favourite pens, and write down a beautiful heading neatly in red, followed by a couple of bullet points summarising the topic. Then you decide to look up something on Google. When you next look at the time, an hour has passed. In that time you have checked your social media, read a few posts, got distracted by an Instagram picture of food, thought about what you might have as a snack later, contributed to a group chat, imagined what you are going to wear to the party on Saturday night, and so on. Then suddenly you wake up and realise that you were distracted – and there is still only one heading and a couple of bullet points on the page.

Most of us spend quite a large part of our lives on autopilot lost in our thoughts, unaware of the sensations in our bodies or what is happening in our environment. Mindfulness is about learning to notice when we are on autopilot, and giving us the tools to switch off autopilot when we choose. It is a way of experiencing the world through awareness of what is happening inside us and around us. Because it is an experience, there is not much point in spending a lot of time describing it in words. It would be like trying to describe the experience of surfing to somebody who has never seen the ocean. Try the next exercise to get your first taste of mindfulness.

Clap Your Hands

- Clap your hands together three times, counting 1 – 2 – 3. Then hold your hands out in front of you a comfortable shoulders width apart.

- Notice what you feel and sense in the palms of your hands. You might notice a tingling sensation, or you might become aware of how hot or cold they feel.

- Now narrow your attention to notice how your thumbs feel. Do they feel different to the palms of your hands?

- Next narrow your attention even further and notice how the top of the little finger on your right hand feels.

- Questions to ask yourself when you are finished:
  - Was I able to direct my attention into each part of my hands, my palm, my thumbs, my little finger?
  - How come I was able to notice what I was experiencing?

The Observer Inside

How did you answer the last question in the *Clap Your Hands* exercise? Here is my answer. There is a part of you that notices everything that you see, hear, touch, taste, smell, think and feel. In mindfulness that part is sometimes called the observer, and it exists in each of us. If your life were a movie, the observer is the part of you that can step back and watch the show. Most of the time we are on autopilot and the observer is not engaged. It is as though we are one of the characters in the movie, caught up in our own drama. When we step into the observer mode we are able to watch the drama unfold rather than get caught up in it.

The observer always lives in the present. One of the problems with autopilot is that we are frequently mulling over the past or predicting the future. This means we miss out on what is happening right now in front of our very eyes. The idea of mindfulness is very simple: just get in touch with the observing aspect of yourself and notice what is happening inside you and around you. Even though it is simple, it is not easy. We get distracted easily, whether it is by the sounds in our environment, interactions with our friends, alerts on our phones, thoughts in our head, or sensations in our bodies. Mindfulness is about developing the skills to get in touch with the observer no matter how strong the distraction.

Mindfulness is a Skill

To become mindful we have to actively focus our attention, and then we have to keep doing it. Mindfulness is a skill rather than a state of mind, and, just like any new skill, we have to practise to become competent. It is a rare genius that can sit down at a piano, kick a football or pick up a golf club and immediately play well. Throughout this book you will find lots of exercises for building your mindfulness muscle.

To make the most of this book it is important to read chapter two, 'Pack Up Your Kitbag'; it explains how mindfulness is beneficial to the teenage brain. In particular, it examines:

- The impact of brain development on emotion regulation
- Why teenagers are programmed to seek novelty without considering the consequences
- The positives and negatives of neuroplasticity
- How mindfulness helps develop the capacity for emotional regulation

Chapters three to five provide the foundation exercises for a mindfulness practice. They teach approaches to working mindfully with emotions, thoughts and rumination. The exercises in these chapters should be practised regularly.

Read in sequence, chapters five to eight round out the basic mindfulness workout described in chapters three and four, and support the development of mental fitness and emotional resilience for the teenage years and beyond. However, it is also possible to dip in and out of these chapters, if there is an area that is of particular interest, as long as the initial work of 'packing up your kitbag' and practising the foundation exercises has been completed.

Just like a physical fitness programme, regular exercise and training is required to become mentally fit and emotionally resilient. Using any exercise described in this book for three to five minutes most days of the week will quickly increase your mental fitness. These exercises will help you develop the following skills:

- Managing your feelings
- Dealing with unhelpful thoughts
- Examining the negative and false stories you tell yourself
- Discovering your values and your strengths
- Learning to be kind to yourself
- Building healthy relationships

The final section of the book provides exercises tailored to common concerns in teenage life:

- Social media and social networking
- Addictive and compulsive behaviours
- Exam and performance anxiety
- Sleepless nights
- Mood busting
- Coping when life gets tough

Our aim is to build and maintain mental fitness and emotional resilience in teenagers, but, in the context of mental fitness, it is also important to address teenage mental health. The book concludes with an overview of how to identify mental health concerns in teenagers and provides suggestions for how to support a teenager who is dealing with a mental health issue.

Before you move on to chapter two make sure to start where you are. Stop for a moment, feel your feet touching the ground, take a breath and notice how it feels to be alive right this minute.

two

Pack Up Your Kitbag

Bob Phillips remarks, 'Teenagers complain there is nothing to do, then stay out all night doing it'. Constant complaints of boredom, reckless behaviour, volatility and moodiness are typical charges that adults make against teenagers. The teenage years are a hectic time for everybody involved.

This chapter helps you pack up your kitbag in preparation for the workouts described in the remaining chapters. It explains some of the reasons why teenagers behave the way they do. When adults and teenagers recognise their behaviour as part of a natural developmental process it reduces conflict and makes life easier for all involved.

This chapter examines:

- Brain restructuring during the teenage years
- The role of dopamine in teenage behaviour
- The importance of social connection in teenage development
- Neuroplasticity and the teenage brain
- How mindfulness supports the development of the teenage brain
- The types of mindfulness exercises in this book

Life on a Teenage Brain

When adults talk to each other about the teenagers in their lives they commiserate about how their once sunny child has morphed into a moody and impulsive teenager, who walks twenty paces ahead of them and claims that everything is 'boring' with annoying monotony. They exclaim that their teenagers never pay attention and have become forgetful and spacey. They worry that their teenagers won't know their boundaries around drugs and alcohol, and bemoan the fact that their child's life force is being sucked out of them by their compulsion for social media and computer games.

Traditionally, raging hormones have been blamed for these behaviours but the latest neuroscience research shows that the teenage years can be better understood in terms of normal changes related to human brain development (Jensen, 2015). 'What brain?' I hear the adults say. 'My teenager's brain went up in smoke on the day they put on their secondary school uniform!'

In fact, the teenage brain is going through a major restructuring process, and it is this more than raging hormones that is responsible for the characteristic teenage behaviour. At times this process appears to create a kind of craziness, but, in terms of human evolution, there is definite method to the madness. Humans have big brains, much too big to be fully formed at birth. The brain continues to develop and mature until about the age of twenty-five. There are two significant spurts of brain development: the first during infancy, and the second from the onset of puberty up to the age of twenty-five.

The brain changes as it grows, so an infant brain is not the same as a teenage brain, and a teenage brain is not the same as an adult brain. The truth is that when an adult exclaims that a teenager should grow up and act their age, the teenager is acting their age; they are acting exactly as their level of brain development dictates. Expecting a teenager to think like an adult is pointless. They can't. They don't have an adult brain.

The Teenage Brain on Stress

In terms of understanding life on a teenage brain, we will take a simplified view of the current neuroscience research into brain development, concentrating on two structures, the amygdala and the prefrontal cortex, and examining their relationship with the autonomic nervous system. The autonomic nervous system is responsible for regulating all the systems in our bodies, including heart rate, respiration and digestion, and it is made up of two branches, the sympathetic nervous system (SNS) and the parasympathetic nervous system (PNS).

The amygdala is a small structure in the brain that acts as a threat detection system. It scans the environment for threats and when it detects a threat it activates an instinctive fight-or-flight or stress response. It works with the SNS to flood the body with adrenaline and cortisol, speed up the heart rate, and tense major muscles in preparation for immediate action. For the sake of evolution, the amygdala is programmed to be very good at detecting threats and it reacts much more quickly to negative information than positive. This stacked the odds in favour of survival in the days when early hominids were prey to large predators. If the amygdala had a motto it would be, 'Act now. Save the questions for later'.

The prefrontal cortex connects to the amygdala. Its job is to provide higher order thinking and executive control. It communicates with the amygdala about how to manage threat. When the threat is not justified, and there is no need for alarm, the prefrontal cortex lets the amygdala know that everything is safe. Then the PNS activates the rest-and-digest or relaxation response, reversing the changes caused by the fight-or-flight response. Digestive enzymes are released into the body, the heart rate drops and muscles relax.

Imagine you were walking through a meadow and suddenly noticed a large rattlesnake in the grass. The amygdala goes on high alert, quickly deciding: rattlesnake = mortal danger

= get out of dodge fast. The sympathetic nervous system activates the fight-or-flight response in readiness for a speedy escape. But then the prefrontal cortex steps in and says: 'Yo, Amygdala, calm down, that is not a snake, it is just a piece of old rope, and anyway St Patrick drove all the snakes out of Ireland yonks ago.' If the amygdala is listening to the prefrontal cortex, it then activates the parasympathetic nervous system to initiate the relaxation response.

Fans of nature shows will recognise both the fight-or-flight and the rest-and-digest response. Imagine a lioness hunting wildebeest on the African plains. When she moves in on her prey, the wildebeest scatter in all directions at great speed, driven by their fight-or-flight response. When the lioness makes her kill and starts to feast, the remaining wildebeest stop running, quickly forget their erstwhile companion, and return to grazing as though nothing happened. The rest-and -digest response lets them know that danger has passed and it is time to chill out and have some well-deserved nosh.

The human brain has the same basic structure as that of the wildebeest, but a larger brain and greater connectivity between the amygdala and the prefrontal cortex mean that humans can make plans. Furthermore, they can process the complex emotional and social information required to engage with other humans to successfully implement those plans.

Back in prehistoric times, when sabre-toothed tigers were snacking on early hominids, this facility for planning, communicating and collaborating saved the day. Hominids joined together in their struggle against large predators. They designed weapons and planned defence strategies and they had the emotional and social intelligence to work together to wage war against the predators. The net result was Hominids: 10; Sabre-toothed Tigers: 0. This is why in today's world our fight-or-fight response is more likely to be triggered by a large, black SUV than a ferocious animal.

One of the most important brain developments during the teenage years is the construction of a complex network of connections between the amygdala and prefrontal cortex. These connections allow the two structures to work together in a cohesive way. While the connections are developing, the teenager's emotional responses to the world are big and intense, and shift dramatically from one stormy emotional state to another. This is in large part due to the amygdala, which runs riot when not under the calming influence of the prefrontal cortex. When the two are fully wired up and working in an integrated fashion, the reasoning processes of the prefrontal cortex calm the overreactions of the amygdala.

The teenage brain is like a home alarm that automatically calls out the emergency services. The amygdala acts as a network of hypersensitive alarm sensors that get activated when toast burns in the toaster, a window rattles in the wind or the family pet jumps against a door. The fire brigade and police arrive with sirens blaring to discover that it was a false alarm. As the neural connectivity of adulthood emerges, the prefrontal cortex acts like the control centre in a monitored alarm. It can check the sensors, evaluate the level of threat and use intelligence to decide what to do.

The Dopamine Effect

Dopamine is a central part of the neural circuitry that creates the drive for reward. That's why it is often referred to as one of the brain's 'happy chemicals'. To help you understand dopamine, think of any activity that you really enjoy, and keep doing, even though it is not very good for you.

Consider my two-year-old daughter. I was a stereotypical health-obsessed mother. I fed her lots of fruit and vegetables, and kept sweets and chocolate out of her diet, working on a hypothesis that she would learn to prefer the natural sweetness of fruit and vegetables to the intense sugar high of chocolate and sweets. Wrong! The very first time she tasted chocolate she went into a trance and a dazed smile spread across her face. Her brain was flooded with dopamine. Ever since then, like chocolate lovers the world over, a quest for another dopamine spike has caused her to seek out chocolate.

In the teenage brain, baseline levels of dopamine are low. This contributes to teenagers' feelings of boredom and frequent bouts of grumpiness. Rewarding experiences act in the teenage brain like chocolate did in my daughter's toddler brain: even small rewards alleviate the monotony of living with low levels of dopamine.

Studies show that teenagers understand the risks and consequences of their behaviour; however, given the immense and epic feelings caused by the dopamine spike associated with a rewarding activity, the risks simply don't compute. This is why teenagers frequently do things that seem stupid and thoughtless. For example, the social reward of partying with a gang of friends outweighs the downside of getting in trouble when they arrive home late to their distraught and angry parents.

This has implications in terms of the teenager's susceptibility to addictive and compulsive behaviours. Until the connections between the prefrontal cortex and the amygdala come online, the amygdala is in a constant state of alarm, creating feelings of high stress. Stress feels bad, and to escape the stress, the reward system drives the teenager towards any activity that releases dopamine to get rid of the bad feelings. Any behaviour or substance that feels good will do. Teenagers can become dependent on anything that feeds their dopamine-hungry reward system, including alcohol, junk food, exercise and even activities as simple as checking how many likes a social media status racks up.

Social Connection

Peer friendships are vitally important during the teenage years. Teenagers have a very strong drive for social connection. They are programmed to start moving away from the adults in their lives and forming bonds with their peers. Think of it like mammals that live in family groups, such as apes, elephants or lions. As the adolescents mature they are expelled from their original family group. Alone, they risk being picked off by a predator so they seek companionship with other adolescent animals, finding safety in numbers.

Fortunately, human adults don't expel their adolescents, but, nonetheless, similar survival instincts create strong drives for social engagement with peers. There is both an upside and a downside to this. The ability to make strong friendships predicts well-being and resilience throughout adulthood. Security and comfort is to be found in groups, and the companionship of peers is vital as children make the transition through adolescence to adulthood.

On the downside, a lack of peer friendship or exclusion from the pack feels like a life-or-death scenario. When a teenager says dramatically, 'I will just die if I can't go to that party', they are actually expressing a legacy of two hundred million years of evolution. It truly does feel like their survival rests on getting to roam with the other young cubs. As adults, we no longer remember the intensity of those feelings so to us it sounds overblown and dramatic.

Teenage brains are programmed to be highly reactive to pack behaviour. Brain scans show that when teenagers are shown a neutral face in a photograph, the amygdala goes into overdrive and they perceive the face as hostile. When similar photographs are shown to adults the rational prefrontal cortex lights up, and adults identify that the expression on the face is neutral. This explains why teenagers are excruciatingly aware of the reactions of their peers and highly dependent on positive feedback and acceptance from them.

Their sensitivity to the reactions of others, combined with the need to conform and be accepted by the pack is where peer pressure can become a problem. Teenagers are more likely to take risks when they are in groups. Behaviours that seem stupid in the cold light of day, even to the teenager, such as driving too fast, drinking excessively or jumping off a balcony into a swimming pool, are easy to engage in when the compulsion to belong works in tandem with the drive towards reward.

Plastic Fantastic
Over the last twenty years neuroscientists have discovered that brain architecture is not fixed, as previously believed. The brain is made up of about one thousand and three hundred grams of tofu-like tissue and has approximately one hundred billion neurons signalling to each other across half a quadrillion synapses. Any mental activity fires neurons and synapses, creating neural pathways or connections. The first time an activity is initiated, a new connection is created. It is as though you walked across a meadow and created a path of flattened grass. If the activity occurs regularly the path becomes more defined, and over time it develops into a country lane, a national route, and ultimately a six-lane superhighway.

This capacity of the brain to adapt and change is called neuroplasticity. One of the earliest studies of neuroplasticity examined the brains of London cab drivers (Maguire, 2006). In order to get their licence London cab drivers are required to commit to memory a complete 'A to Z' of London streets, and must pass a sequence of progressively difficult oral tests referred to as 'the knowledge'. On average it takes four years to pass. Functional MRI studies of their brains reveal that their hippocampus, an area of the brain associated with memory and spatial awareness, is substantially thicker than average.

During the teenage years the brain is particularly malleable. On the plus side, this plasticity means that teenagers can acquire new and complex skills with great ease. They can learn to kitesurf, solve quadratic equations, skateboard, play the ukulele, adapt to new technology and become fluent in Japanese, while their parents struggle to turn on the TV with a new remote control and rely on their phone calculator to divide the dinner bill.

The brain operates on a use-it-or-lose-it basis. This means that consistent practice is required to maintain any network of connections. Teenagers have direct experience of this if they have ever asked a parent for help with calculus or wanted guidance on metaphysical poetry. Most adults forgot about calculus and John Donne's poetry straight after they walked out of their Leaving Cert exams, and since then they have made no attempt to rebuild those connections!

There is one significant downside to neuroplasticity: the brain learns from negative experiences just as easily as it does from positive experiences. On the journey to adulthood the last brain systems to mature are those that regulate emotion and provide insight and judgement, yet those are the very systems required to navigate the complex social interactions and the pressure to perform facing teenagers. If a teenager is feeling excluded socially or consistently feels unable to deal with pressure, the brain can end up building a six-lane superhighway that ends in a spaghetti junction of worry, low mood, compulsive behaviours and dependency on substances. This is why mental health problems that emerge in adolescence can persist into adulthood if they are not addressed early.

Exercising the Brain Through Mindfulness

The main construction job in the teenage brain is connecting up and integrating the frontal cortex with the amygdala. Unfortunately, this job does not progress in a neat, linear fashion. Brain development is like releasing a new computer or phone operating system: in the early versions there are lots of bugs and glitches to be ironed out but with every release exciting new functionality is added, old bugs are fixed and new bugs surface.

One of the main goals during this phase of development is to bring the prefrontal cortex online so that it is available to moderate the alarm system of the amygdala. In the early stages of development it is like streaming movies over the internet. Occasionally the connection drops and all you see is that infuriating circling going around and around in the centre of a frozen image.

The mindfulness exercises in this book support teenage brain development in a number of ways;

- Each exercise starts with a focus on lengthening the exhalation. Exhaling activates the PNS, telling the amygdala that everything is safe. By repeatedly stimulating the PNS the brain develops a six-lane superhighway that leads to a landscape of calm and relaxation instead of a spaghetti junction of worry, low mood, compulsive behaviours and dependency on substances. This inoculates the brain against future mental health issues.

- All the exercises increase activity in the prefrontal cortex while reducing activity in the amygdala. This is accomplished in a number of ways: noticing and labelling thoughts and feelings; answering questions that require self-reflection; writing about negative experiences or distressing feelings; using visualisation.

There are three categories of mindfulness exercise in this book:

CORE EXERCISES

- Equivalent of abdominal exercises in a physical workout
- Build the core strength required for good emotion regulation
- Form part of a daily mindfulness workout
- Can be done anywhere and at anytime
- Do not require a quiet space

REFLECTIVE EXERCISES

- Encourage active self-reflection
- Require a pen and paper
- Require a quiet place free from distraction

TARGETED EXERCISES

- Equivalent of exercises targeting a specific muscle group in a physical workout
- Target specific areas such as social media usage, sleep and exam pressure

To take full advantage of the plasticity of the teenage brain, the exercises must be practised regularly. But they don't need to be practised for long. Choose any exercise and do it for three to five minutes most days. Mindfulness fits perfectly into daily life, but you have to remember to do it. Here are some ways of keeping mindfulness in mind as you go about your day:

- Pause for a moment between transitions in your day. A transition is any time you finish one activity and move to the next. Use the *Mindful STOP* at the start of every class, before you eat a meal, or every time you finish an activity.

- Choose a specific time everyday to do one to two minutes of mindfulness: before getting out of bed, while travelling to school, or before settling down to watch a box set.

- Download a mindfulness app on your phone and use it any time you are hanging around with nothing to do, like sitting on a bus, or waiting to be collected.

- When you are walking spend a minute or two noticing your environment, listening out for sounds, and observing what is happening around you.

- If you work out in a gym, do at least one workout a week mindfully. Arnold Schwarzenegger recommends putting your 'mind in the muscle' and this is one of my favourite ways of incorporating mindfulness into daily activity.

Summary

- The teenage brain is going through a major restructuring process that makes it difficult for teenagers to regulate their emotions.

- The teenage brain has a low baseline level of dopamine, and this leads teenagers to prioritise reward over risk.

- Teenagers have a strong drive for social connection. They are programmed to start moving away from the adults in their lives to form close bonds with their peers.

- Teenagers can take advantage of neuroplasticity to acquire new skills during their teenage years, but the same neuroplasticity makes teenagers vulnerable to mental health problems.

- Mindfulness supports the development of emotion regulation for long-term mental fitness and emotional resilience.

three

Ride the Emotional Roller Coaster

JK Rowling says, 'You couldn't give me anything to make me go back to being a teenager. Never. No, I hated it.' Most adults remember the teenage years as an emotional roller coaster ride that was at times thrilling and exciting but frequently confusing and distressing. Riding the emotional roller coaster that is adolescence involves learning to handle the chaotic feelings that are a daily part of life.

It focuses on:

- Understanding the difference between emotions and feelings
- Identifying and labelling emotions and feelings
- Becoming aware of any strategies used to avoid difficult feelings
- Soothing intense feelings with mindfulness

Emotions

A lot of the time the words 'emotions' and 'feelings' are used interchangeably, but there are some important differences. Emotions are automatic responses in our body and brain that prompt us to act in a way that enhances our chances of survival, whether that is moving towards good things or escaping bad things. Recent research suggests that there are four basic emotions: happy, sad, fear/disgust and fear/anger (Jack, 2014).

Emotions come in strong, peak quickly, but have a relatively short life. They are felt in the body in the form of changes in breathing, heart rate and the digestive system. Neuroanatomist Dr Jill Bolte Taylor suggests in *My Stroke of Insight* that the brain releases chemicals into the body triggering the emotional reaction, but within ninety seconds the reaction is over. For teenagers, life is lived on an emotional roller coaster. Emotions change with dizzying speed due to the lack of connectivity between the amygdala and prefrontal cortex (see in chapter two, 'Life on a Teenage Brain').

A feeling, on the other hand, is how the brain makes meaning about an emotion. While the basic emotions are instinctual, and common to all human beings, and probably to other mammals, the meanings the emotions take on in the form of feelings, thoughts, actions and mood are based on a mixture of life experience and individual temperament.

Imagine two teenagers, John and Sarah, who have just seen a disapproving expression on the faces of their friends. Remember that teenagers are particularly susceptible to the opinions of others (see in chapther two, 'Social Connection').

Emotion	Feelings/Thoughts/Actions/Mood
John reacts with fear	His fear turns to hostility
	He has the thought 'nobody is going to treat me like that'
	He gets into a fight
	He remains in an irritable mood for the rest of the day
Sarah reacts with sadness	Her sadness turns to dejection
	She has the thought 'I am no good and nobody likes me'
	She remains in a low mood for the rest of the day

It would be nice to imagine that happy emotions always lead to good things, and often they do, but for teenagers there are some downsides due to the dopamine effect (see in chapter two, 'The Dopamine Effect'). Imagine two teens, Eva and Liam. Eva is getting ready with her friends before going out. She notices approving looks on her friends' faces when she has a drink. Liam is on vacation with his friends and sees approving looks on his friends' faces when he jumps off a rock into the sea.

Emotion	Feelings/Thoughts/Actions/Mood
Eva reacts with happiness	Her happiness turns to excitement She has the thought 'everybody loves me when I am drinking' She drinks more She remains high until her mood crashes later that night
Liam reacts with happiness	His happiness turns to excitement He has the thought 'they will think I am even cooler if I jump from a higher rock' He climbs onto a higher rock He remains excited until he falls and injures himself

The trick to dealing with powerful and overwhelming emotional states is recognising when we need to hit the pause button. This gives the prefrontal cortex time to catch up with the amygdala so that we can choose a response to the emotion rather than simply reacting. It allows our internal observer to step in so that we can be alongside our feelings rather than caught up in them. Let's look at what happens in the cases of John and Sarah if they hit the pause button.

Emotion	Feelings/Thoughts/Actions/Mood
John reacts with fear but hits the pause button	He notices the fear and pauses He thinks about the level of danger and realises he is safe He does nothing He remains in a good mood for the rest of the day
Sarah reacts with sadness but hits the pause button	She notices the sadness and pauses She thinks about ways of soothing herself She reaches out to a friend and talks about how she feels She remains in a pensive mood but notices some hopefulness too

The *Mindful STOP* provides a way to hit the pause button. It is the most important exercise in this book. Consider it as the mindfulness equivalent of the abdominal crunch. Practising the *Mindful STOP* regularly will give you core strength, mental fitness and emotional resilience. Use it anytime and anywhere. Nobody needs to know that you are doing it. Do it whenever you feel worked up, distressed, anxious or overwhelmed. Take a moment to do it before you enter a stressful situation; talking to somebody you don't know well, speaking up in class, sitting a test, making a phone call, or speaking to an adult.

The acronym STOP helps you remember how to hit the pause button:

- **Stop for a moment**
- **Take a breath**
- **Observe what is happening**
- **Pursue your best course of action**

Mindful STOP

- **Stop**

  Pause for a moment and put your attention on your feet. Notice the sensation of your feet touching the ground.

- **Take a breath**

  Gently and slowly focus on exhaling, take a pause, and then allow your next breath inwards to fill and expand your chest and tummy.

- **Observe**

  Get in touch with the observer in you.
  Observe what is happening inside you. Notice the sensations in your body, paying attention to your heart beating in your chest, and the sensation of air entering and leaving your body.
  Observe what is happening around you. Notice any sounds in the environment. Look around you and notice what you see.

- **Pursue your best course of action**

  Make a choice about what you want to do next. Calming your emotions gives you space to choose a skilful response to the situation that has got you hot and bothered.
  - Maybe the emotion has calmed enough and there is nothing you need to do
  - Maybe you want to walk away from the situation
  - Maybe you want to say something about what is happening
  - Maybe you want to reach out to a loved one for comfort

Feelings

Feelings are more complex than emotions and they can hang around a lot longer than ninety seconds. Feelings are like a weather system. A low-pressure weather system brings dark clouds that loom overhead in a threatening way. Everything looks grey and dull, but it doesn't stay that way forever. At some stage the sun comes out from behind the clouds and immediately everything looks brighter and more beautiful. One thing we know for certain is that the weather will change. The same is true for feeling states, but it takes considerably longer than the ninety seconds of an emotion. Feelings can loom overhead for hours and even days.

Feelings are more complex than emotions. We often have more than one feeling at the same time. A really simple example is when you are about to do something new or different. You might feel both excitement and anxiety at the same time, excitement about the chances of it going well, and anxiety because you don't know how it will turn out.

Just like the weather, we tend to rate feelings as 'good' or 'bad'. It is certainly true that some feelings are more pleasant to experience than others. Who doesn't like the sunshine feelings of joy, love, excitement and curiosity? These feelings are associated with good times and they create pleasurable sensations in our body. We often try to avoid feelings like anger, sadness and jealousy, labelling them as 'bad' and pretending they don't exist.

How do you feel right now? Often when people are asked this question the answer is 'grand', 'fine', 'OK' or 'not so great'. These answers don't come anywhere near describing the complexity of feelings. Nor do they help communicate feeling states to others. Back to the weather analogy: a weather forecaster that described the weather as 'grand', 'fine', 'OK' or 'not so great' probably would not last long in the job.

Not knowing how to identify and express feelings makes it difficult to communicate with friends and family. The first step in communicating feelings is to be able to identify them. The Sami, who live in the Artic regions of Norway, Sweden, Finland and Russia, have as many as one hundred and eighty words to describe snow and ice. Just as people have developed lots of words to describe local weather conditions, there is a vast array of words to describe feeling states. Most people are not particularly good at linking these words with how they feel in the present moment. As well as helping to communicate feelings, identifying and labelling feelings has been shown to soothe difficult feelings and increase positive effects. The next exercise helps you practise labelling your feelings.

Identifying Feelings

- Gently and slowly focus on breathing out, take a pause, and then allow your next breath in to fill and expand your chest and tummy. Do this one more time, and then allow your breathing to return to normal.
- Use the list of feelings in Table 1 on the next page to help you identify all the feelings you might have in the following situations. It helps if you imagine a time when you found yourself in a similar situation.
  - You didn't win an important match
  - You get a good grade on a test and your teacher says well done
  - You get a bad grade on a test and your parents tell you that you should work harder
  - One of your friends ignores you
  - Your best friend wins a special prize
  - Your brother/sister is allowed to do something that you are not allowed to do
  - You are not allowed to go to a party
  - Somebody does something thoughtful and kind for you
  - You say something mean about someone
  - You do something nice for someone
  - You meet somebody new

Accused	Discouraged	Horrified	Remorseful
Adored	Disdain	Hostile	Resistant
Afraid	Disgust	Hurt	Revengeful
Aggravated	Eager	Ignored	Sad
Alarmed	Ecstatic	Impatient	Self-conscious
Alone	Embarrassed	Impressed	Shocked
Angry	Energetic	Infuriated	Silly
Anxious	Excited	Inhibited	Spiteful
Ashamed	Exposed	Insecure	Stunned
Astonished	Fearful	Insignificant	Stupid
Bitter	Frightened	Insulated	Surprise
Blue	Frustrated	Joyful	Suspicious
Bored	Glad	Lost	Tender
Cautious	Gloomy	Loving	Tense
Cheerful	Grateful	Miserable	Thankful
Content	Grieving	Motivated	Trapped
Cross	Guilty	Nervous	Ugly
Curious	Happy	Offended	Unaccepted
Defensive	Hateful	Optimistic	Uncomfortable
Delighted	Heartbroken	Outraged	Used
Depressed	Helpless	Petrified	Useless
Devastated	Hopeful	Pleased	Warm
Disappointed	Hopeless	Rebellious	Worthless

Table 1: Feeling Words

It can be useful to do this exercise with a friend or family member. You will probably find that you share some of the same feelings, but also feel quite differently about some things. A shy introverted person will feel anxious and self-conscious about meeting somebody new, whereas a gregarious extrovert will feel excited and optimistic. Don't assume other people feel the same way as you do, and when you are hanging out with your friends, try to be mindful of the different reactions they have. Doing so can help you understand your friends better and reduce conflict in your relationships.

The Great Feelings Escape

Sometimes people try to avoid the feelings they find unpleasant, such as sadness, fear, guilt, anger, disgust and shock. Unfortunately, this doesn't work very well. Life consistently throws up difficult situations that result in unpleasant feelings. Friends say hurtful things and we feel angry and sad. Relationships break down and we grieve the loss. We make a joke that falls flat and we are smothered in embarrassment. We fail at something and we feel shame.

When we avoid unpleasant feelings they create pressure inside. You know those sachets of tomato ketchup you get with fast food. They are incredibly difficult to open, even at that little dashed line that supposedly indicates where to tear. Then when you manage to create a little tear the ketchup squirts out and lands everywhere but on your fries. This is a bit like what happens when feelings build up inside: sometimes they squirt out over our friends and family.

Cian was coming to see me because he was experiencing low mood and outbursts of anger. His story illustrates the way feelings can 'squirt out' when they build up inside. During the day he had stuffed down a number of difficult feelings and in the end they squirted out over Ashling, his little sister.

I had a bad day at school yesterday. During the first class of the day my teacher got on my case because I forgot to do my homework. He gave me a detention. It was so unfair. He is an idiot, and if he wasn't so boring I wouldn't forget to do the homework! At lunchtime I tried to chat up Anna and she ignored me. I said to my friends that she is not all that and she should be so lucky. I said it loud enough for her to hear! Then when I got home my mum had a go at me. I went upstairs to play *Call of Duty* and the stupid Wi-Fi was down. Then

Ashling came into my room. She wanted a red pen or something. I was so mad I threw my pencil case at her.

People use a variety of strategies to manage unpleasant feelings. The list in the next exercise provides a number of possibilities. Cian did the following:

- Blamed other people
- Said mean things about other people
- Avoided spending time with people
- Distracted himself by using the internet and social media
- Picked fights

Do the next exercise to figure out the strategies you use to avoid your feelings. Any time you notice yourself avoiding your feelings use the *Mindful STOP* to help you pause and notice the feelings. Ask yourself the question, 'What would it be like if I allowed these feelings to be here?'

Avoiding Feelings

The table below lists a number of strategies commonly used to manage unpleasant feelings. It is not exhaustive; you might be able to think of some more. Take some time to note any strategies that you use. If you come up with more strategies add them to the list. See if you can work out which feelings you avoid by using each strategy. Think about friends and family members and see if you know which strategies they use.

Ways of avoiding feelings	I do this	The feelings I avoid
Avoid spending time with other people		
Blame other people		

Break things		
Daydream		
Drink alcohol		
Eat junk food		
Exercise too much		
Lie		
Listen to music really loudly		
Make a big deal out of feeling sick or hurt		
Obsess about something else (like how you look, what you should have said, or how well you do in school)		
Pick fights with people		
Play computer games excessively		
Pretend you don't care		
Restrict the amount of food you eat		
Say mean things about other people		
Steal		
Take drugs		
Tease other people		
Try not to be noticed		
Try to please other people		
Use the internet and social media excessively		
Watch TV excessively		

Get Friendly with Your Feelings

Have you ever noticed how it feels when somebody acknowledges your feelings? The heat and charge goes out of them, and something in you settles and feels more comfortable. Feelings hide because they have been ignored for so long but when we allow ourselves to be curious in a friendly way we create space for them to come out. Once we are on friendly terms with the feelings they don't seem so enormous or distressing, just like the monster under the bed that turns out to be a much-loved but forgotten teddy bear.

In the next exercise you will learn how to get friendly with your feelings. In this exercise you are listening on the inside, sensing inside yourself and then waiting to see which feelings come to say hello. The feelings might let themselves be known in a number of ways:

- Sensations in your body, particularly in your stomach, chest and throat
- An image in your mind that represents your sense of the feelings
- A sensation like a weight on your shoulders, a band tightening around your head or a knot in your tummy
- Descriptive words or phrases that pop into your head

The main thing with this exercise is to allow the feelings come to you. Give them time and space to arrive. The feelings need to be sure that you are going to listen.

Get Friendly with Your Feelings

- Gently and slowly focus on breathing out, take a pause, and then allow your next breath in to fill and expand your chest and tummy. Do this one more time, and then allow your breathing to return to normal.

- Bring to mind a recent situation where you lost your cool, got very down on yourself, or felt embarrassed. Notice the dominant feeling you have about this situation, maybe anger, sadness or shame.

- Make an intention to welcome all the feelings about this situation.

- Repeat the phrase 'Something in me feels _____' using the dominant feeling you identified. For example: 'Something in me feels embarrassed.'

- Sense inside and notice any sensations in your tummy, chest or throat. Let your hands go gently to anywhere that feels as though it could do with some attention. Offer to be alongside the feelings. Have a sense of breathing in some tender, loving care to that place. Be patient while you wait and see what feelings emerge.

- **Questions to ask yourself when you are finished:**
  - What feelings did I notice? If it helps use the list of feelings in Table 1.
  - How do I normally avoid these feelings?
  - What might I do differently in the future if I find myself in a similar situation?

Use this exercise any time you notice yourself using one of your avoidance strategies to check in and discover the complex mixture of feelings you are experiencing.

Cian's Story
We met Cian earlier in this chapter. After he told me the story of how he threw his pencil case at his sister Ashling we

used this exercise to help him get better acquainted with his feelings. The dominant feeling he had at the time was anger, but as he gave the other feelings space this is what he noticed.

Cian had been speaking very fast and seemed angry.

> **Iseult:** You are speaking very fast right now. It is like something in you is angry?
>
> **Cian:** Of course I am angry!
>
> **Iseult:** And you are *feeling* angry. If you slow down just a little, can you sense inside what it is like when something in you feels angry? Do you notice any sensations in your body, maybe in your throat, chest or tummy?
>
> **Cian:** I notice something in my stomach. It is like a kind of fizzing. And then it moves up into my chest, like it wants to burst out, like a shaken-up bottle of soda.

Cian put a hand gently on his stomach and his chest and imagined breathing into those areas.

> **Cian:** It's like if the lid stays open, just a bit, the fizzing is not as bad. Now I just feel bad, not mad.

Cian is silent for a moment.

> **Cian:** I feel sad.

Over time Cian started to recognise the 'fizzing' feeling as a mixture of anger, shame and sadness. He was able to use the *Mindful STOP* to insert a gap between the 'fizzing' and his reaction. He found he had fewer outbursts of anger and he could choose other ways of soothing himself.

Summary

- Strong emotions last for about ninety seconds but the feelings, thoughts, actions and moods that follow hang around for longer. Using the *Mindful STOP* hits the pause button on your emotions so that you can choose how you want respond.

- Feelings are more complex than emotions. People use lots of different strategies to avoid their feelings. Many of these strategies are not helpful in the long term.

- Mindfulness gives you a way of getting friendly with your feelings, so that you can develop helpful strategies for taking care of them, and no longer need to avoid them. Any time you notice yourself avoiding feelings practise *Get Friendly with Your Feelings*.

- Practising the *Mindful STOP* and *Get Friendly with Your Feelings* regularly helps you develop emotion-regulation skills.

four

Get Friendly with Your Thoughts

In his book, *10% Happier: How I Tamed the Voice in My Head*, Dan Harris describes mindfulness as 'the skill of knowing what's happening in your head at any given moment without getting carried away by it'. In reality we all have a soundtrack going on in our minds, kind of like a radio chattering away in the background.

This chapter focuses on:

- Becoming aware of the soundtrack in your head
- Observing the tone of your thoughts
- Noticing when you are getting carried away by thoughts
- Getting on friendly terms with your thoughts

The Human Brain is a Thinking Machine

Homo sapiens, our species, evolved a complex and rather large brain. So when Carl Linnaeus named the species in 1758 he chose a Latin name that means 'wise man' or 'knowing man'. Over the millennia, our capacity to think has led to many great discoveries and inventions: fire, the wheel, the combustion engine, the suspension bridge, the horseless carriage, penicillin, the computer, the smartphone and the internet, just to name a few. Thinking is a good thing most of the time.

Our brains are thinking machines. They produce an endless stream of thoughts throughout the day. All over the internet there are articles stating that we have approximately seventy thousand thoughts a day. I have recited that factoid countless times in mindfulness workshops but I thought I better fact-check it if I was going to put it in a book. The only scientific research I found comes from the National Science Foundation in the US and it estimates that the average person thinks about twelve thousand thoughts a day. It pays not to believe everything you read on the internet!

Many of those twelve thousand thoughts are thoughts we had previously, and many are thoughts we will almost certainly have again. When not generating thoughts about useful, interesting or earth-shattering topics, our brains offer up some pretty repetitive, negative and, quite frankly, uninteresting material. I am a fairly typical person and this is a good example of what goes on in my head:

> I am going to really focus today. I want to get this chapter finished. I'd love a latte now. I wonder if they have those croissants they had yesterday. I am going to get so fat if I keep eating those croissants. I'll go to the gym later. Maybe I'll see that cute trainer there. I better not have a croissant. I love the banana bread, probably healthier than the croissants. I forgot to feed the dog.

Even though I like to think of myself as an intelligent and interesting person this is an accurate reflection of the background chatter that goes on in my head. Most people I know agree that the chatter inside their heads is similarly banal.

The truth is that just about everyone talks to themselves but not everyone is aware of it. We have grown up with our brains chattering like a radio in the background. Occasionally we tune in to the thoughts and hear what is being said but a lot of the time we don't notice.

At other times we become completely caught up in our thoughts. Think of it like being hooked by a TV series on Netflix: you finish an episode and even though you have watched four already, and you were definitely going to bed after the second episode, you are completely hooked and you just have to watch the next episode. Our thoughts can hook us like this and we find it hard to switch into observer mode.

In the next exercise you are going to work on noticing your thoughts and listening to the chatter in your brain without getting hooked by it. Start by practising the exercise for as little as three minutes, but over time try to increase the length of time you practise.

Clouds Go Sailing By

- Gently and slowly focus on breathing out, take a pause, and then allow your next breath in to fill and expand your chest and tummy. Do this one more time, and then allow your breathing to return to normal.

- As you relax start to create a picture in your mind. Imagine yourself lying in a field on beautiful summer day, feeling relaxed, with nothing to do but look at the sky. You are lying on a soft blanket and you can hear the sound of the grass rustling in the wind. Looking up you see a beautiful vivid blue sky. Clouds drift lazily by. Imagine the warm sun shining on your body, helping you feel even more relaxed.

- When a thought enters your mind imagine it is like a cloud in the sky, gently drifting by. Allow the clouds to drift at their own pace. Don't try to speed them up or slow them down. Some of them will hang around, and that's OK; eventually they will drift away.

- Notice what your mind is saying. Perhaps it says things like 'I am useless at this', or 'I'm so bored', or 'This is stupid', or 'I would prefer to stick hot needles in my eyes than sit here doing this'. These are thoughts; imagine them as clouds, and let them drift away.

- As you do this exercise you might find yourself getting hooked by your thoughts and unable to picture the sky. That is okay. As soon as you realise that you are hooked, just say 'hooked' to yourself and focus on your breathing. Then go back to imagining yourself lying in the field looking up at the vivid blue sky.

- If you find yourself having a painful or distressing thought, just acknowledge it. Say to yourself, 'I notice myself thinking this painful/frustrated/angry/sad thought', and then allow it to drift away like the clouds.

- **Questions to ask yourself when you are finished:**
  - If my thoughts were like the weather, what kind of weather system was I experiencing?
  - Which kind of thoughts were the 'stickiest'? Sticky thoughts are those that hang around for a long time or keep popping up again and again.

Not everybody likes using the image of clouds in the sky. Use any image that works for you. Other examples include sitting by a river watching leaves float downstream, watching trains entering and leaving a station or watching images on a computer or television screen fading away. I suggest clouds because I find it gives people a way of visualising the kinds of thoughts they are having and notice what mood comes with those thoughts.

The Tone of Our Thoughts

During the last exercise you will have noticed somewhere in the region of forty to one hundred and thirty-five thoughts, depending on how long you spent doing it and the speed at which your brain was producing thoughts today. When you listen to those thoughts it is as if something inside is involved in an inner dialogue. Don't worry, this kind of dialogue is totally normal. It is not a sign of madness! Most people do it.

When people in real life talk to us, we don't only listen to the words, we pay attention to their tone of voice. When your mother says, 'I really like it when you leave your shoes in the middle of the kitchen floor', it is quite likely that her tone of voice lets you know that, in fact, she really means, 'It is totally driving me crazy that you always dump your stuff all around the house I have spent hours cleaning.'

The tone of voice people use affects your mood. Maybe you were in a good mood as you walked into the house, but the tone of voice your mother used put you in a bad mood. Inside your head you might have said something like, 'There she goes again, always moaning on about stuff. I can't wait to grow up and move out of this house.'

Did you know that your thoughts have a tone of voice too? The tone of your thoughts can affect your mood. When the tone is unfriendly you will probably find yourself in a bad mood and when it is friendly you will generally feel good about life.

In the next exercise you are going to examine the tone of your thoughts. We will use an imaginary scenario where you have planned to hang out with a friend, but the friend is very late. For the purpose of the exercise, you will rate the tone of your thoughts on a scale of unfriendly to friendly. The following diagram gives you some adjectives for unfriendly and friendly tones. The list is not exhaustive – you can add any other adjectives that make sense to you.

Unfriendly	Friendly
Sarcastic	Excited
Irritated	Strong
Horrified	Agreeable
Hurtful	Kind
Critical	Cheerful
Resentful	Animated
Agitated	Calm
Stroppy	Laid-back

The Tone of Thoughts

- The tone of our thoughts impacts the way we think and feel about situations. In this exercise you are going to imagine a scenario with a friend and see what kind of tone your thoughts take. There are three parts to the exercise. Measure the tone of your thoughts on a scale of Unfriendly to Friendly at the end of each part of the exercise.

- For readability I have used names in the text, but the exercise will be more powerful if you imagine real-life friends and an actual place where you hang out.

- At the end of each part answer the following questions using the scale of unfriendly to friendly:

Unfriendly	Friendly

- What kind of explanations am I coming up with for my friend's lateness?
- What thoughts am I having?
- What tone are those thoughts taking? Mark it on the scale.
- How am I feeling towards my friend? Mark it on the scale.

■ Part One

You have arranged to meet your friend Jennifer in a cafe. She is thirty minutes late and you are sitting there alone, wondering whether to buy another coffee or leave. You feel kind of stupid and imagine people wonder why you are sitting there on your own like a loser. You have been texting Jennifer and you have heard nothing back. Imagine what it feels like to be sitting alone in a cafe. Take a minute to imagine what it feels like to be stood up by your friend. Now answer the questions listed above.

■ Part Two

You call your friend James about the situation. James doesn't like Jennifer as much as you do. He starts criticising her and saying she shouldn't treat you like that. He also mentions how annoying her laugh is and that he hates the way she shows off in class. Finally, he says that he notices that sometimes she raises her eyes to heaven when you make a joke. Take a minute to imagine how you feel after talking to James. Now answer the questions listed above.

■ Part Three

Now imagine you get a text from another friend. It explains that Jennifer was injured while playing sports and has been taken to hospital. Take a minute to imagine how you feel and what you are thinking after hearing this explanation for Jennifer's lateness. Now answer the questions listed above.

How the Tone of Our Thoughts Impacts Us

In the first part of the exercise you have no factual information about why your friend is late. Without being consciously aware your mind has taken a position. The tendency is to come up with negative interpretations. Even though we often interpret situations negatively the facts can change our perspective and as our perspective changes so too does the tone of our thoughts.

Our brains are a little like the internet. They are filled with lots of information, thoughts, ideas and beliefs. Some of these are useful, valid, true and important. Others are less so, just like that fake factoid that I mentioned at the beginning of the chapter, the one that suggests that we have seventy thousand thoughts a day. It is a good idea to notice our thoughts, and then take some time to check how true they are. It is also good to notice how situations, and the things other people say, are affecting the tone of our thoughts.

When I do *The Tone of Thoughts* exercise with groups most people tell me they have unfriendly thoughts when they imagine the first part of this situation. Those thoughts get even less friendly after listening to the negative perspective of another person. Unfriendly thoughts impact how we perceive a situation, but when new facts emerge they challenge our perceptions.

Just as you should be careful of believing everything you read on the internet, you should be careful of believing everything you think. Your thoughts are often not the best guide to understanding the situation. Check in and see what kind of tone your thoughts are taking. If they are unfriendly, pose the question, 'How would I see this situation if my thoughts were a little more friendly right now?'

Caitlin's Story

Caitlin came to see me because she was experiencing low mood and was finding it difficult to keep her friendships. She had started avoiding school. She was very sceptical about how mindfulness could help her. During our sessions, when I noticed her thoughts were hooking her, I would ask her to take a breath, and pause, and notice the chatter in her brain. At first she asked how 'just breathing' was going to help her friendships, but over time she found that it did make a difference.

One day she was very distressed about an incident that happened earlier with one of her friends. She had been sitting in the canteen when she saw Deirdre come in. She waved to Deirdre but Deirdre ignored her and sat at another table. Caitlin heard the group at the table laugh as Deirdre sat down. She told me that 'she just knew that they were laughing at her because of her hair'. She had dyed her hair the day before and it was a bit of a disaster.

Here are the thoughts Caitlin noticed:

- Deirdre doesn't want to be my friend anymore
- My hair is horrible and now they are all laughing at me
- I am totally ugly
- I am so stupid
- Nobody likes me
- I always lose my friends
- I will never have a boyfriend because I am such a loser
- I am going to be lonely forever

First I asked her to notice the tone of her thoughts. She said the tone was unfriendly. Next I asked her, 'What kind of unfriendly?' She noticed that they were critical and angry.

Then I asked her to take three mindful breaths and pose the question, 'What would it be like if my thoughts got a little more friendly right now?'

She noticed a shift in the tone of her thoughts, and along with the shift in tone came a change in perspective. Some other possibilities entered her mind. It was possible that Deirdre had not seen her. It was unlikely that one bad dye job was going to result in all the dire consequences her mind was predicting. She was feeling vulnerable because she was embarrassed about her hair and this had contributed to the unfriendly atmosphere in her mind.

Summary
- Our brains produce as many as twelve thousand thoughts a day. We spend quite a lot of time hooked by these thoughts and end up distracted and unable to focus.

- Mindfulness helps you notice when your thoughts have hooked you. By repeatedly noticing that you are caught up in your thoughts and returning to the present, you develop your ability to focus and concentrate. Practising *Clouds Go Sailing By* regularly is a good way of building this mindfulness muscle.

- The tone of your thoughts colours your perception of what is happening. By helping you to notice the tone of your thoughts, mindfulness helps you challenge unfriendly and unhelpful thoughts. You can check the tone of your thoughts anytime during the day when you notice that you are hooked by your thoughts.

five

Tall Tales and Fake News

'Truthiness' is a word coined by Stephen Colbert, a US comedian, on his political satire show *The Colbert Report*, and means something that seems and feels like it is true, even though it is not. All good fake news stories have a ring of truthiness.

Did you know that our brains are the greatest purveyors of fake news ever? And, just like some people reading stories in their Facebook feed about a polar bear stranded on an iceberg that floated onto a Scottish island or Prince Harry's secret wedding, we believe the stories our brain serves up.

This chapter focuses on:

- Identifying the tall tales and fake news our brains tell us
- Looking at how these tall tales distort the truth
- Turning down the volume on the stories

The Brain is a Storyteller

In the last two chapters we separated out feelings and thoughts as though they were two distinct processes. This provides a good starting point for noticing, recognising and identifying different feelings and thoughts. In reality the picture is a little more complex. Feelings and thoughts combine to create our experience of the world. Sometimes feelings trigger a particular sequence of thoughts, and other times a thought triggers a particular set of feelings.

As we become familiar with the twelve thousand thoughts our brain serves up each day we start to notice that among these thoughts are stories that we tell ourselves over and over again. These stories can be about what type of person we are, what other people do to us or how the world treats us. Our brains are creative so the stories can be about anything at all. At the same time our brain is a bit like a dotty great aunt. Once it finds a story it likes it never tires of telling it, over and over, again and again, and so it goes.

When our brain starts telling a story it goes around and around in our heads, like an earworm, one of those annoying songs you hear on the radio that plays on repeat in your head the whole day long. If the story is about something fun and happy then you should enjoy it until you need to focus on something important. Unfortunately, many of the stories our brain tells us are sad, negative and critical. It is like having a harsh commentator in the background describing our every move.

Our brain is programmed to focus on what is wrong due to an evolutionary negativity bias. In order to pass on their genes, our ancestors had to make critical life-or-death decisions many times a day. Are those red berries poisonous or possible super foods? If I eat them will I die and prevent my descendants from colonising the planet and developing the internet? Nowadays our daily dilemmas tend to be more concerned with how many hearts were clocked up on a social media update, or how we might just die if we don't get the latest trainers.

Due to this negativity bias, our brains have a lot of opinions about what is 'good' or 'bad'. If a human brain were a salesman it could sell American-style fridge-freezers to Eskimos. That is how good a job it does getting us to believe its evaluation of a situation. When it comes to listening to our brains we tend to believe it is telling the truth, the whole truth and nothing but the truth. We end up buying an oversized fridge-freezer despite the fact that we have acres of sub-zero tundra outside the front door.

We rarely share these stories with anybody else so the stories go unchallenged. It is a strange thing; we are both storyteller and captive audience at the same time. Many of the stories can be summed up with a short synopsis such as 'You are useless', 'Nobody likes you', 'There is something wrong with you', 'It is not your fault', or 'They should not have done that to you'.

Matthew lived with social anxiety. He was naturally shy and as he progressed through secondary school he found himself less able to engage in social situations with his peers. When I asked him why he felt anxious about attending school this is the story he told me:

> I hate the way people stare at me when I come into the room. I know I stand out like a sore thumb. When I have to talk to somebody I know my voice will get strangled in my throat and nobody can hear me. I never have anything intelligent or funny to say. My face always goes red and my heart starts racing. I end up speaking too fast and my thoughts are jumbled, or I can't finish a sentence because my voice gets so stuck. I know everybody thinks I am really stupid. They think I am boring and they don't like me.

The story is powerful and convincing. His body reacts as though the exact situation he is describing is happening right now. He starts to feel down on himself and is convinced that everybody in the world thinks he is dull and stupid. The story is accompanied by a compelling image of his discomfort. He can see his red face and almost feel his sweating palms. The images in his head and the feelings in his body confirm the truth of the story.

On the other hand, all I see is a guy sitting in a chair, hunched up, making no eye contact and mumbling. It is hardly surprising then that people in his life find it difficult to relate to him. It is not because they think he is stupid or find his jokes dull. It is because he gets so caught up in this story that he is not able to be present to his friends. When somebody is caught up in listening to an internal story, they can't connect with other people. Spending time with a person who is caught up in a story is like spending time with someone who is talking on his or her mobile phone instead of taking part in the actual conversation.

The stories we tell are not always about ourselves. Sometimes they are about our friends, our parents or other people we know. Caitlin, who we met in chapter four, frequently gets angry and blames other people when things go wrong in her life. She finds it difficult to maintain friendships and feels very lonely and isolated. She frequently tells me stories where she is the victim of a nefarious plot:

> I am never speaking to Susie again. She is so mean. I told her something, totally in private, on chat, and she took a screenshot and shared it with Anna-May and Mary. How dare she do that to me? Our chat was private. We are supposed to be friends and that is how she treats me.

As I enquired further into what had happened it transpired that Caitlin had been saying spiteful things about Anna-May and Mary to Susie, and she had been spreading rumours about them on a wider group chat. Susie was caught in the middle and had decided to share what was being said. Caitlin is so caught up in the story of how other people have wronged her that she can't see her own contribution. These stories of victimhood sabotage her relationships.

Both Matthew and Caitlin are swept along by the story. The feelings generated are intense and all-consuming. In turn, the feelings feed the narrative of the story and make it more dramatic. The story is never subjected to any challenge because the mind has a captive audience of one. That is not to say that everything in the story is untrue. It is possible that some people do notice that Matthew appears a bit awkward but that doesn't mean they automatically despise him. Similarly, in Caitlin's case, it may be true that other people contribute to the situation, but by consistently blaming everybody else for what happens in her life, she avoids having to examine her own actions.

Most of the stories our brains tell us have the following characteristics:

- No matter how bad the story makes us feel it is almost impossible to let it go; it keeps going around and around in our head.

- The story seems to describe the only possible version of events; it doesn't allow space for other people's perspectives.

- It feels like something that is happening right now even though it often concerns a past event or something that may or may not happen in the future.

- The stories are absorbing to the point that we don't notice what other people are feeling or doing. We imagine they are reacting as though they are a character in our story.

- The stories are peppered with words like 'always', 'never', 'should', 'can't', 'no one', 'everyone', 'must'.

In the next exercise you are going to write down one of the stories you frequently tell yourself. If one doesn't come to mind immediately, watch out over the next few days and see if you notice one and then complete this exercise.

Tall Tales

- Bring to mind a story that your mind often tells you. Now get in touch with a recent situation where your mind went into overdrive telling you this story. Visualise as many details of the situation as you can. What happened? How did it make you feel?

- Write down the story in a stream of consciousness. Don't worry about spellings, grammar or punctuation. This is for your eyes only. Spill all your thoughts onto the page. Write on one side of each page only, leaving the other side blank. Keep writing until you find that the story has gotten really boring and repetitive and it seems like everything there is to say has been said.

- Gather the pages together and fold them in half so the story is on the inside and you are left with blank paper on the outside. Write 'This is a story I tell myself'. Put the pages down, a distance away from you.

- Bring your attention to your body, your feet touching the ground, and feel how the chair supports your weight.

- Focus on your next out breath, seeing if you can make it a little longer and slower. Breathe this way for three to five breaths.

- Ask yourself, 'In what ways is this story helpful?' Sense deep inside yourself to see what answer emerges.

- Ask yourself, 'In what ways is this story unhelpful?' Sense deep inside yourself to see what answer emerges.

- **Questions to ask yourself when you are finished:**
  - What feelings are associated with this story?
  - Does the story have the same hold over me now that I have written it down?
  - How often do I tell myself this story?
  - How often do the details of the story change?

Turning Down the Volume

Noticing the stories we tell ourselves is a great first step. It helps us see when we are overthinking or obsessing about life events and situations. In psychology we call this rumination, and people who ruminate are vulnerable to low mood and worry. They tend to be consumed by the negative things that happened to them in the past and feel hopeless about the future. Rumination is one of the habits of the mind that is most likely to lead to mental health problems, particularly depression and anxiety.

It is important to find a way of turning down the volume so the story becomes less compelling and there is space to choose a more positive outlook. Every time the volume is turned down on one of these stories the brain starts to build a pathway out of the rumination (see chapter two, 'Plastic Fantastic'). Here are some suggestions for turning down the volume. Experiment until you find the approaches that help you the most.

- Imagine the story is playing on a big-screen TV and pick up an imaginary remote control and hit mute.
- Imagine a silly-sounding cartoon character telling the story. How dramatic does it sound told by Dora the Explorer, SpongeBob SquarePants, Dee Dee from *Dexter's Lab*, or one of the Little Ponies?
- Sing the story in your head to the tune of a jolly song like 'Jingle Bells' or 'Happy Birthday'.
- Challenge the story, asking, 'How does this help me right now?' If it does help you in the short-term investigate if it is going to make your long-term future better.
- Say to yourself something like, 'Here I go telling the story of why I will never _____, I have heard it before, and I know how it ends.'

■ Put your thoughts on pause by using the *Mindful STOP* and see if you can figure out what way your brain is distorting the situation. Below is a list of the most common thought distortions our brains use. Thought distortions are filters that prevent us from seeing the truth of the situation. See if any apply in the stories you regularly tell yourself.

All-or-Nothing
All-or-nothing thinking is seeing things as all bad or all good, rather than recognising the complexity.

> Daragh was at a party. He was having a brilliant time. He loved the music and everything was great fun. Then he tried dancing with a girl he fancied and she ignored him. He decided the party was useless, everybody was boring and he had never heard such rubbish music in his entire life.

Negative Filter
The negative filter involves scanning for the negatives and blocking out the positives.

> Sophie was looking through her social media feed. Lots of her posts had likes but when she saw one negative comment she obsessed over it and forgot about all the likes.

Emotional Thinking
Emotional thinking is the belief that feelings define the truth about a situation.

> Theo is a good student but gets very anxious about exams. After every exam he worries that he answered

the questions incorrectly and is convinced he has not done well. He feels like a failure. When the exam results come back he discovers he has done well. Nonetheless every time he allows his feelings of anxiety to prevent him from making a reasonable assessment of his performance.

Perfectionism

Perfectionism is the belief that if things don't turn out perfectly it is not worth doing them at all.

Daniel believed he had to get all As, be a great athlete and be the most popular guy in school. He frequently felt disappointed in himself. He gave up running because he didn't come first in a race. He procrastinated about his study. If he wasn't going to do brilliantly, he would rather say it was because he hadn't studied than because he was not good enough to get an A.

Catastrophising

Catastrophising involves viewing minor upsets as complete disasters.

Emma got a C in a class test. She knew this meant that she would barely pass her end of year exams, eventually fail her final exams, never get a job and ultimately become homeless.

Mind-reading

Mind-reading is the belief that it is possible to read other people's thoughts.

Leah sent her boyfriend a text. An hour later he had not replied. She was convinced he wanted to end the relationship so she decided to break it off with him before he got the chance. It turns out that he left his phone at home and did not see her text.

Matthew's Story

We met Matthew earlier in this chapter. He had developed crippling social anxiety. When he was younger he had been somewhat shy, but he had always had a small group of friends with whom he felt comfortable. As social anxiety took a grip on his life he avoided all contact with his friends. He felt very lonely and isolated. Even imagining basic social contact from asking a shop assistant for help to texting a friend brought on an anxiety attack. He stopped going to school.

In one session I asked him to write down the story he was telling himself when he had the urge to skip school. We saw it earlier in this chapter. He chose a title for the story, 'The Story of My Shocking Embarrassment'. During the following week I asked him to notice every time he started telling himself the story. His task was to focus on using the *Mindful STOP* and get in contact with the internal observer by saying, 'Here I am telling myself "The Story of My Shocking Embarrassment again".' Then he was to experiment and see which techniques helped him turn down the volume.

Being mindful of the story helped him to challenge the story in the present. Were people really staring at him? Was he the only person that sometimes struggled to say something? Was everybody else super witty and intelligent all the time? Would it be a disaster if he made a joke and it fell flat?

As he became less caught up in the story he found that he could challenge the truthiness of the story:

- Sometimes people laughed at his jokes
- Sometimes other people said stupid things but nobody seemed to mind

- Other people seemed uncomfortable at times, he wasn't the only one that felt awkward
- Even though he was concerned about his face going red it never actually happened
- People didn't seem to notice his discomfort; they were caught up in their own concerns

His social anxiety didn't disappear overnight, but he started to find ways of dealing with it, and was able to return to school.

Summary

- Our brains tell us stories over and over again. These stories can be about what type of person we are, what other people do to us, or how the world treats us. In psychology this is called rumination. Rumination is one of the mind habits that leads to and maintains depression and anxiety.
- The stories involve various kinds of thought distortion. Thought distortions are filters that prevent us from seeing the truth of a situation.
- Mindfulness helps you move into observer mode so that you can find ways of turning down the volume and reducing rumination.

six

Value Finding and Strength Spotting

Teenagers face many complex dilemmas on the journey to adulthood. As they gain independence from their family they need to develop their own value system to help them make wise choices; however, they are given very little opportunity to develop their own personal code. In addition, they are consistently ranked against other teenagers and end up feeling 'not good enough'. This constant comparison game leaves them feeling under-resourced. As Simon Sinek says, 'Spending too much time focused on others' strengths leaves us feeling weak. Focusing on our own strengths is what, in fact, makes us strong.'

This chapter focuses on:

- Developing a personal code through discovering inner values
- Identifying and developing personal strengths
- Using mindfulness to feel resourced by savouring strengths and values

Values for Inner Guidance

Children are given a lot of ideas about how to behave in the world: tell the truth; say sorry when you do something wrong; share with your friends; don't cheat at games; do your best. These values come from parents, teachers and society. Children don't question them. They accept them and more or less try to live up to them.

Teenagers venturing out into the world find themselves in new and tricky situations, having to make increasingly complex choices about the right way to behave. They find the values handed to them in childhood are no longer fit for purpose in the complex social world in which they live.

- What do you do when a friend is drinking too much?
- Is it okay to lie to avoid disappointing your parents or hurting a friend's feelings?
- If your best friend is suicidal, is it okay to betray his or her trust by telling an adult?
- If you know your friend's girlfriend is cheating on him, should you say something?

Not only do values help teenagers make decisions when faced with complex dilemmas, they also help them reach their goals. Johnny has a goal of getting high grades in his exams. Even if that goal is realistic, the chances of him arriving there are slim unless he has a value of working consistently. When Johnny has to choose between knuckling down and studying or watching the next episode of his favourite box set, values can help him make a good choice.

If the exams are six months away, it is difficult to stay motivated by the goal of getting good grades. The destination is too far away. If Johnny gets hooked and watches the complete box set, he can convince himself that he still has time to make up for the missed study. If, instead, he uses the value of working consistently, he can make a choice that moves him closer to his destination. He can decide to watch an episode after he has completed his study for that day.

Goal	Value
To get high grades in exams	To study consistently
To be super fit	To eat healthily and exercise regularly
To be the best	To do your best
To be a great friend	To act with kindness even when you feel angry or hurt
To win at sports or play a musical instrument brilliantly	To commit to practising regularly

Not everyone has the same values, or cares about the same things, so it is important to develop an individual personal code. Using mindfulness helps you to tune in to your values. It can be useful to reflect on personal values within six dimensions using the following questions:

Family	• What sort of son/daughter, brother/sister do you want to be? • How would you behave towards other family members when you are being your best self? • What qualities do you believe are important in family relationships?
Friendships and Social Life	• If you were the most loyal, best friend ever, how would you behave towards your friends? • What qualities do you believe are important in a friendship? • What qualities would you like to bring into your friendships?

School	• What do you enjoy about learning? • If you were the best student ever, how would you behave in school?
Recreation and Fun	• How do you bring fun and joy into your life? • How do you contribute to bringing fun and joy into your relationships?
Health and Well-being	• What is important in looking after your health (sleep, diet, exercise, etc.)? • What do you do to relax and unwind?
Spirituality and Citizenship	• What is important to you in spirituality and religion? • How would you like to contribute to your community? • How would you like to contribute to the environment? • How would you like to contribute to making the world a better place?

For example, consider the dilemma about what to do if your best friend is suicidal. Perhaps the following values are important to you:

- Being loyal
- Not betraying secrets

But when you ask yourself the question 'If I was the most loyal, best friend ever, what would I do right now?' then the answer becomes a little clearer. Of course loyalty and keeping secrets is important, but a best friend makes sure their friends get help when they are in deep distress.

The next exercise helps you discover the values you hold dear. Use it to develop your own personal code and do it any time you are facing a dilemma or are having difficulty staying on track.

Values Finder

- Gently and slowly focus on breathing out, take a pause, and then allow your next breath in to fill and expand your chest and tummy. Do this one more time, and then allow your breathing to return to normal.

- Close your eyes. Set a timer for sixty seconds and for that time gently pose the question: 'What is my deepest value in _____?' (Select one of the areas listed in the table above)

- Notice any thoughts that come up in response to the question, but don't let yourself become hooked or distracted by them. Keep bringing your attention back to the question again and again. Wait for an answer to rise up from deep inside you rather than actively thinking about what the answer should be.

- When the timer goes off write down a word or short phrase that captures that value.

- When you have finished writing, set your timer again. Repeat the exercise two more times, each time writing down the values that emerge. The same value might come up, or other values might come into focus. There is no right or wrong answer.

- At the end of the three rounds look at the words and phrases. If there is more than one, circle the one that seems truest for you at the moment. Allow yourself to be surprised.

- Finally, set the timer one last time. This time repeat the circled word or phrase silently while you imagine yourself making choices based on this value. Notice how it feels when you imagine yourself living by this value.
- **Questions to ask yourself when you are finished:**
  - Is this value important to me?
  - When I act from this value do I feel good about myself?
  - Would I be pleased if people I respect and like knew that this was important to me?
  - Does this value fit with my vision of the person I want to be?

Cian's Story

We met Cian in chapter three. He was having difficulty with his temper and his relationship with his parents had deteriorated. There was constant shouting and fighting. When I first talked to him about his values in the dimension of family he was quite dismissive.

> Well of course I know I should respect them and I shouldn't shout at them. Everybody knows that. But they should do the same and not shout at me.

With a little persuasion, he decided to give the *Values Finder* a try. He was surprised by what he found. The most important value that emerged was love. I suggested that when things were getting heated he might try hitting the pause button with the *Mindful STOP*, and then pose the question, 'What would it be like if I had a little more love right now?'

Cian continued to find his parents annoying, but on the occasions that he could find a little more love, it was easier for him to step back and disengage from the conflict. As he stepped back, his parents calmed down and their relationship began to improve. Getting in touch with his values was not the only mindful practice he used. You can read more about how he changed his relationship with his parents in chapter eight.

Strength Spotting

Every person has different strengths and weaknesses, things they do well naturally and things that take time and repeated practice to do at all. When working from a place of strength people feel energised and positive. Studies in positive psychology have found that people who tried using their strengths in a new way each day for a week were happier and less depressed six months later.

The teenage years are a tough time when young people are consistently under pressure to perform academically, in sports and socially with their peers. Most of the time they receive criticism that corrects what they do wrong rather than feedback that celebrates what they do well. When the focus is on our weaknesses we end up feeling frustrated, tired, hopeless and useless. It is no wonder that so many teenagers report high levels of anxiety and depression.

When the focus shifts to thinking about the things a person does well they usually feel motivated, invigorated and engaged. This is exactly the feeling we have when we are using our strengths. It is a feeling of being resourced. We work faster and more effectively and we feel good. Mihaly Csikszentmihalyi coined the phrase 'flow state' for this feeling. It is the same feeling that athletes describe as 'being in the zone'.

We experience flow states under the following circumstances:

- We want to do the activity
- The activity requires some skill

- We find the activity challenging but success is within our reach
- The activity requires concentration and focus

Teenagers are often forced to do activities where they feel no sense of flow. They are so far out of the zone they might as well have been transported to a galaxy far away. Here are a few of the activities that made me feel out of the zone when I was a teenager: solving quadratic equations; remembering where to use subjunctive verbs; learning dates of rebellions and land acts; cross-country running; anything to do with geography.

Unfortunately, mindfulness can't make us geniuses at things that don't come naturally to us; however, it can help us to get better at noticing and developing our strengths. Think of strengths like charms or talismans that can support you in every area of your life. But in order to use them you have to know that they are at your disposal.

The next exercise helps you identify how you feel when you are doing things that play to your strengths. It comes in two parts. First, imagine doing something that you are no good at, and then imagine doing something that consistently makes you feel energised and happy. The contrast will help you understand how good it feels when you are working from your strengths. In psychology we often call this a feeling of being resourced. Most of us are not in the habit of thinking about things we do well so sometimes we need help. Here are some questions to help you get started:

- Can you remember a time when you felt really proud of yourself, even if other people didn't think it was a particularly big deal?
- What activities make you feel energised and glad to be alive, even if you don't think you are particularly good at them?

- What activities do you remember particularly enjoying when you were younger?

To help spark your imagination, here are some examples that teenagers have shared with me. As you will see, they run the gamut from the mundane to the downright odd, but they share a common characteristic: the person describing the activity got really excited when they were telling me about it. They loved doing it and they were visibly animated while they were telling me about it. This is a key indicator that they were using their strengths.

- Finding new music on YouTube
- Playing skipping games in the yard when I was six
- Kicking a football around on the street
- Doing my friends' make-up before we go out
- Spelling tests (no really, one person did say that!)
- Playing rugby
- Teaching my dog tricks

Strength Spotting

- Gently and slowly focus on breathing out, take a pause, and then allow your next breath in to fill and expand your chest and tummy. Do this one more time, and then allow your breathing to return to normal.
- Think of something you are not good at, but nonetheless, find you have to do occasionally. Imagine yourself doing it in as much detail as you can.
  - What does it feel like?
  - What kind of stories do you tell yourself when you are doing this?
  - How is your energy as you think of yourself doing this?

- Think of something you really enjoy doing. You don't necessarily have to think it is important or a great achievement. Imagine yourself doing it in as much detail as you can.
  - What does it feel like?
  - What kind of stories do you tell yourself when you are doing this?
  - How is your energy as you think of yourself doing this?

- **Questions to ask yourself when you are finished:**
  - What personal qualities do I use when I am doing the thing I really enjoy? Use the list in Table 2 below as a starting point, but don't limit yourself. You might think of other qualities, or you could ask an adult that knows you well to help you spot your strengths.

Adventurous	Driven	Intuitive	Optimistic
Charming	Efficient	Kind	Outgoing
Compassionate	Enthusiastic	Level-headed	Passionate
Creative	Focused	Loyal	Persistent
Curious	Funny	Meticulous	Persuasive
Decisive	Imaginative	Observant	Punctual
Diplomatic	Intelligent	Open-minded	Relaxed

Table 2: Personal Qualities

Values and Strengths Training

The *Values Finder* and the *Strengths Spotter* help you discover your values and strengths. You can revisit these exercises any time you feel challenged by a situation in your life, or you are worried about what direction to take. Consciously remembering your values and strengths helps you stay on track and brings a sense of feeling resourced.

It is important to incorporate your values and strengths in daily life. The best way to do this is to choose a particular value or strength to work with over a number of weeks;

then, on a daily basis, when you hit the pause button with the *Mindful STOP*, ask yourself the question, 'What would it be like if I had a little more _____ right now?' Simply asking this question keeps you connected to your values and your strengths, and helps you make skilful choices about how to deal with everyday dilemmas.

Mia's Story

Mia had been experiencing low mood for months. She was failing academically. The one thing in life that she really enjoyed was gymnastics. She competed regularly in competitions but only occasionally won medals. She had been good at gymnastics but not great. Nonetheless, she had loved doing it, and had practised up to ten hours a week until an injury forced her to stop.

In our early sessions I found it very hard to engage Mia. She wasn't rude, in fact quite the contrary, she was very polite, but everything was said in a quiet monotone. She sounded disengaged and her tone was heavy. She didn't hate school. She liked her teachers well enough. She tried to study but she found it difficult to concentrate. She told me she had never done well academically, but now she couldn't keep up and was failing. She was afraid she would never achieve anything in life. There where times in the initial sessions that it felt like the psychotherapy might not achieve anything either!

I asked her to describe what it felt like when she was doing her gymnastics. The guidelines were the same as in the *Strength Spotting* exercise: to remember and then tell me about it in the present tense, as if she were doing it right now. She described how it felt when she was doing the bars, her favourite rotation:

> I am looking at the bars. Like really looking at them. I can see the high bar, but I am focused on the low bar

for my mount. I jump and swing up. I love the feeling as my body swings through the air. And then there is a moment of preparing for the dismount. It's a great feeling when I stick it, but even if I don't it's okay. It is flying through the air that I really love.

She immediately started to speak more clearly. Instead of short, hesitant sentences her speech was lively. There was energy in her voice. Her description was rich and multi-layered.

I asked her to have the sense of breathing those feelings into her body and notice what it was like. Then I asked if there was anything in her current life that gave her the same feelings. She said the only time she felt good was the two hours a week she spent coaching gymnastics. She had once again returned to her monotone. The feeling of being resourced had evaporated. Again, I asked her to talk about coaching as though she were doing it right now.

The little ones are kind of mad, always running around. So I have to get them to pay attention, but there is no point shouting at them or being too strict, or they get kind of nervy, and then they make mistakes. So I make them do silly competitions during the warm-up, like who can keep smiling while doing thirty V-Sits. That kind of thing. And then when it comes to teaching them skills I break it down really simply for them, step by step, so they really get all the parts of the move.

Once again, Mia sounded animated and alive. I spotted a couple of strengths immediately, but it took a little longer for Mia to recognise them. Often that is the case. We discount things we are naturally good at and don't see how we could use them elsewhere in our lives. Here are the strengths we ended up agreeing on:

- Explaining things to other people so they find it easy to understand
- Using her sense of humour to inspire people
- Bringing joy and laughter into people's lives

We talked about how she could start using these strengths to feel more resourced in her academic work. I asked her to use her strength of explaining when she was studying. Rather than trying to learn things by rote she was to imagine how she might explain the topic to somebody who knew nothing about it. In addition she was to try to find something funny to say about it. Slowly she started to feel more engaged in her schoolwork and stopped failing.

Now when I am doing my English essays I imagine Miss O'Brien has never even heard of *Pride and Prejudice* and I am trying to explain all the stupid things that made it really difficult for Elizabeth Bennet and Mr Darcy to get together. You know something, I know I am never going to be brilliant at English, but that's OK, because I am going to a personal trainer. My training gym is going to be a fun place to be and I am going to post step-by-step guides for working out on YouTube!

Mia stopped comparing herself to others and focused on her strengths. She started to believe in herself and could see herself in the future accomplishing her goals.

Summary

- Values help us to make wise choices and keep us on track when we face dilemmas or distractions.

- We feel motivated, invigorated and engaged when we are using our strengths. Consciously working from our strengths can protect us against anxiety and depression.

- Our values provide inner guidance on how to reach our goals. Our strengths keep us on track when the going gets tough.

- Daily mindfulness helps us connect with our values and strengths and creates a sense of feeling resourced in the face of life's challenges.

seven

Taking Care of Number One

Many people live with a background chatter of harsh criticism and negative judgement in their heads. Doctor Kristin Neff, who has researched self-compassion extensively, says, 'The biggest reason people aren't more self-compassionate is that they are afraid they'll become self-indulgent. They believe self-criticism is what keeps them in line' (quoted in Parker-Pope, 2011). Neff's research shows that self-compassion is associated with high levels of happiness, optimism, initiative, curiosity and agreeableness. When we take care of number one we have the energy and compassion to care for others.

This chapter focuses on:

- The problem with self-esteem
- The reasons why self-compassion works where self-esteem fails
- Using mindfulness to develop self-compassion

The Problem with Self-Esteem

All my clients, adults as well as adolescents, tell me they want to work on their self-esteem. This is not surprising. Studies have shown that people with high self-esteem have more self-confidence and feel better about themselves than people with low self-esteem. As a result, hundreds of books have been published on ways to increase self-esteem. Parenting manuals teach parents how to raise children with high self-esteem, and schools have implemented programmes that aim to raise the self-esteem of all children.

People seem to believe that self-esteem is a characteristic that can be measured on a scale. If their self-esteem score increases, they expect to feel good about themselves and their life. The truth is that levels of self-esteem are not fixed; they fluctuate based on life circumstances, successes and failures, and, more unpredictably, on mood.

For many years we have been led to believe that if we raise children to have high self-esteem they will feel happier and be more successful in life. Research finds that although high self-esteem creates pleasant feelings and leads to more initiative taking, it does not lead to higher academic grades, good job performance or lasting happiness. The truth is that many highly successful people have low self-esteem. In private they feel like imposters in their life and worry incessantly that some day they will be found out. Conversely it is assumed that teenagers who take drugs, drink or become sexually active at a young age, do so due to low self-esteem. Interestingly, these problem behaviours are more related to difficulties with emotional regulation than low self-esteem.

One of the problems with the pursuit of high self-esteem is that it is predicated on success and specialness. We try to build self-esteem by telling teenagers they are special and great, but then for everybody to have high self-esteem it would mean that everybody would be above average. Basic maths dictates this cannot be true. We expect our teenagers to do brilliantly – but where are our own display cases full of trophies and awards? Imagine the pressure they feel!

It is particularly difficult for teenagers growing up in today's culture. They are praised for their success in academic, sporting and artistic pursuits; however, self-esteem plummets when high results in at least one of these areas are not achieved. In order to feel above average they have to compare themselves to others, constantly seeking to be better than their friends. This is when the internal self-critical voices get very shouty. If you put what these critical voices said in a text it would be in all caps: 'YOU TOTAL IDIOT, HOW COULD YOU HAVE MADE A STUPID MISTAKE LIKE THAT? YOU ARE NEVER GOING TO AMOUNT TO ANYTHING.' It is not surprising that people feel bad when the trolls in their head are at the ready to criticise everything they do.

Instead of trying to get self-esteem to do the heavy lifting we need to focus on building our self-compassion muscle. Sometimes people are afraid that if they are kind to themselves they are letting themselves off the hook and avoiding responsibility. They believe that they will only perform well if they crack the whip internally. But this is a form of deep unkindness. When I ask if they would speak to a friend or a small child the way they talk to themselves the answer is always no. Here are some of the reasons people give me for why it is okay to be unkind to themselves:

- If I am not hard on myself I will keep making mistakes
- The only way to be good at things is to be tough on myself
- I am so lazy I need to give myself a good kick to get myself going
- I don't deserve kindness because I am such a loser

Learning to have self-compassion is about accepting that it is human to make mistakes. We all do things we feel bad about. We all say things that we later regret. We all make choices that are not fully in line with our values. Beating ourselves up doesn't change what happened. My model for self-compassion is the Satnav Chick, the calm lady who helps me find my way when I am driving. The Satnav Chick is very kind and she never gets judgy or harsh. When I make a wrong turn, and, as my poor beleaguered passengers will tell you, it happens often enough, the Satnav Chick just says, 'recalculating'. Then a moment later she calmly lets me know what to do. She does not say, 'STUPID WOMAN, YOU DID IT AGAIN! NO MATTER HOW MUCH WARNING I GIVE YOU, YOU STILL TAKE THE WRONG TURN!' Self-compassion works in the same way to prevent people from getting lost in self-critical cul-de-sacs and rumination roundabouts. Instead of getting caught up in regret, cut yourself a break and recalculate.

Do the next exercise twice. The first time imagine a situation where you messed up badly, the kind of situation that makes your toes curl with embarrassment when you remember it. The second time imagine a situation where you feel you did something well, a time where no matter the outcome you feel like you can hold your head high. The exercise will help you to understand how your self-esteem and your capacity to be kind to yourself fluctuate.

Self-Esteem vs Self-Compassion

- Use the following meters to measure your self-esteem and your self-compassion during this exercise:

Self-Esteem Meter

Low   High

Self-Compassion Meter

Easy   Difficult

- Gently and slowly focus on breathing out, take a pause, and then allow your next breath in to fill and expand your chest and tummy. Do this one more time, and then allow your breathing to return to normal.

- Remember the situation in as much detail as possible, making the memory as vivid as possible. Take a few breaths where you really feel as though you are breathing in the feelings that this situation brings up. Make the feelings as vivid as possible.

- How high is your self-esteem right now? Mark it on the self-esteem meter.

- Repeat the phrase 'When I imagine this situation I love and accept myself'. Mark how easy it is to say that you love and accept yourself on the self-compassion meter.

- Questions to ask yourself when you are finished:
  - Are my self-esteem scores the same for both situations?
  - How easy do I find it to love and accept myself when things are not going according to plan?

Why Self-Compassion Works

Doctor Neff's research on self-compassion shows that it offers real advantages over self-esteem. In one study people were asked to imagine being in an embarrassing situation; for instance, forgetting their lines during a performance in a show, or missing a shot in an important game. Self-esteem seemed to have very little impact on people's reactions. Those with low self-esteem and those with high self-esteem were equally likely to go on a self-critical tirade, having thoughts like 'I wish I could die' or 'I am such a loser'. People who scored high on self-compassion were able to counter these self-critical responses with thoughts like 'Everybody makes mistakes sometimes' and 'In the long run, this doesn't really matter'.

Overall, the research shows that people with high levels of self-compassion are less likely to compare themselves to others and feel less need to retaliate when they believe somebody has insulted them. They are less likely to insist they are right and others are wrong. On the other hand, people who have high self-esteem without self-compassion often need to defend their position, because seeing themselves as wrong negatively impacts their sense of self-esteem.

Self-compassion does not depend on feeling special or above average to feel good. It allows us to let go of the comparison game and stop competing in a never-ending race. We come to accept ourselves in our messy, fragile, beautiful magnificence, discovering that sometimes things go brilliantly, other times disastrously, and, often, things just go reasonably well. No matter what happens, it is possible to feel okay, and feeling okay most of the time is better than feeling brilliant occasionally and rubbish the rest of the time. One of the simplest ways of thinking about self-compassion is that it is the belief that we are 'good enough' just the way we are. This is in contrast to high self-esteem, which demands that we are special and fantastic, and forces us into the comparison game.

Training the Self-Compassion Muscle

When working with self-compassion it helps to have an image in your mind. I often suggest to my clients that they watch a scene from the movie *The Help*, where Aibileen, a maid and nanny, regularly repeats the following mantra to the unloved four-year-old girl that she minds, 'You is kind. You is smart. You is beautiful.' Aibileen wants the little girl to grow up believing in herself.

Rather than giving airtime to our self-critical inner voices, we need to develop an inner Aibileen who speaks kindly and lovingly to us, and this next exercise helps you do that.

Choose somebody compassionate, a person on whom you can rely, to speak kindly to you and about you. It can be somebody from your life such as a parent, a grandparent, or a teacher, a compassionate being such as Jesus or a spiritual leader such as Gandhi or the Dalai Lama. The most important thing is that you choose a person or being to whom you feel some connection.

Self-Compassion Strength Training

- Gently and slowly focus on breathing out, take a pause, and then allow your next breath in to fill and expand your chest and tummy. Do this one more time, and then allow your breathing to return to normal.

- Picture your compassionate being in your mind. Imagine them smiling at you with loving eyes. Imagine that they are wishing you well. Maybe they are saying words like 'May you be loved just as you are. May you be happy just as you are. May you find peace and calm even in tough times'.

- Notice if you feel comfortable accepting this person's kindness towards you. Notice if you have any resistance to their good wishes. Imagine letting their good wishes in and see what that feels like.

- Take a moment to see if there are other words that you would like to or need to hear, and imagine your kind being saying these words to you.

- On each breath in imagine you are breathing these good wishes into your heart. Try to smile inwardly at yourself the way this being is smiling at you.

- **Questions to ask yourself when you are finished:**
  - How do I feel after doing this?
  - Could I accept good wishes from this person? If not, perhaps you need to do some *Self-Compassion First Aid* before doing this exercise again.

Self-Compassion First Aid

When something goes wrong or we make a mistake our amygdala goes crazy (see chapter two, 'Life on a Teenage Brain'), sounding a klaxon, while we are taken over by strong emotions like anger and shame. These emotions surge through our body and are so overwhelming that self-compassion goes out the window. At times like this we miss out on the opportunity to practise self-compassion by avoiding our feelings. If you find yourself doing any of the following things, try some self-compassion and see what happens:

- Thinking obsessively about the situation, going over it again and again in our head
- Getting angry with somebody else and blaming them
- Blaming yourself
- Making bargains about how you won't ever end up in a situation like this again

At times like this it can be hard to find self-compassion through imagining our friendly, compassionate being. We need our frontal cortex to come online to do the visualisation required for that exercise, but the amygdala has hijacked the connection to the frontal cortex. In this situation some self-compassion first aid is required. This exercise combines a technique used for working with trauma, aimed at calming amygdala-based reactions with self-compassion.

Self-Compassion First Aid

- Cross your arms over your chest so that your right hand is over your heart and your fingers are just below the collarbone. Imagine your thumbs form the body of a butterfly and your hands are the wings.

- Begin to tap, first on one side, and then on the other, as though the wings of the butterfly are flapping. Focus on your breathing while you tap rhythmically to a marching beat. Keep tapping for about one minute.

- Say the following phrase to yourself, 'Even though this happened may I completely love and accept myself' and see what it feels like to imagine loving and accepting yourself.

- At first you might notice that it does not feel possible that you would ever completely love and accept yourself. Keep tapping and see if that changes.

- When you feel calm, stop tapping and notice how you feel about yourself. For most people the strong emotions decrease, creating space for some self-compassion to emerge.

Ciara's Story

Ciara came to see me for issues relating to disordered eating. Like many of my clients with this issue she had been a perfectionist since early childhood. The problem with perfectionism is that it puts people into a no-win situation. Perfection is impossible so the perfectionist always feels like a failure. Self-compassion is the only true antidote to perfectionism, yet it is the hardest medicine to take when afflicted by perfectionism!

Ciara believed that the only way that she could achieve perfection was to mercilessly beat herself up when she 'messed up'. For Ciara 'messing up' was getting less than an A on a class test, taking a bite of a biscuit or going out without perfect make-up. In fact the list of things that counted as 'messing up' was endless and exhausting, and I often felt like going straight to bed when I imagined trying to live up to her levels of perfection.

When we first started looking at the idea of self-compassion she was not interested. It was clear to her that even one single gram of self-compassion would start her on a very slippery slope towards complete mayhem. Recovery from disordered eating creates a huge dilemma for perfectionists. On the one hand, a part of the person wants to follow the eating plan perfectly, while another part wants to maintain what is seen as a 'perfect' weight, and so refuses to follow the eating plan.

Ciara was very committed to her recovery so she agreed to try the self-compassion practices. In the early days she found that *Self-Compassion First Aid* helped her stay on track.

> I don't think there will be a time when I completely love and accept myself, but even though that tapping stuff seems stupid, it does calm down the noise in my head, and both eating-disorder me and non-eating-disorder me can agree to eat something.

Later in her recovery she was able to start the *Self-Compassion Strength Training*. She had a very close relationship with her grandmother and at times during her early childhood she had felt that her grandmother was the only person in the world who loved her.

> When I started imagining Nana smiling at me I didn't want her to look at me. I was afraid she would see how useless I am. But then I remembered her smile and how she always told me I was so brave and I knew she would love me even when I mess up. I hate to admit it, but it is getting a little bit easier to like myself. Sometimes when things are bad now I imagine her smile and I feel like I can get through the day.

I don't want to suggest that this was an easy journey for Ciara, or that mindfulness magically cured her disordered eating, but when she looked back on what had helped her the most, she said that learning to be a little kinder to herself was what had started her on the road to recovery.

Summary

- High self-esteem is contingent on success and does not guarantee happiness or self-confidence.
- Self-compassion counters critical inner voices and allows us to step away from the comparison game.
- Practising self-compassion regularly supports good mental health and research shows self-compassion is associated with high levels of happiness, optimism, initiative, curiosity and agreeableness.

eight
Navigate Relationships Mindfully

Relationships are both the primary source of joy and the primary source of stress in most people's lives. If you don't believe me take a moment to review the last week. Try to remember the three most stressful, annoying or upsetting situations you found yourself in. Then count how many of these stressful incidents were related to your feelings about another person.

We can reduce relationship stress by changing how we communicate with and respond to others. As William James said, 'Whenever you're in conflict with someone, there is one factor that can make the difference between damaging your relationship and deepening it. That factor is attitude' (James, 1890).

This chapter focuses on:

- Discussing the importance of teenage friendships
- Examining why relationship stress arises
- Learning mindful approaches to improving communication and reducing relationship stress

The Importance of Teenage Friendships

Peer relationships are incredibly important to teenagers (see in chapter two, 'Social Connection'). In their growing independence from their family, teenagers turn to their peers as their first line of support in times of distress or worry. Acceptance by peer groups is vitally important. Teenagers often show their allegiance to a particular group by the way they dress, the activities in which they participate and the celebrities they follow. These choices symbolise their increasing independence from their family while giving them a sense of security and acceptance as they develop new and important peer relationships.

Dismissing these choices as attempts to fit in or as peer pressure undervalues the importance of peer relationships in a teenager's life. Adolescent peer groups are different to the friend groups of younger children. They are closer and more tightly knit. Teenagers share very deep feelings with each other and the shared emotional vulnerability creates a deep intimacy among the group. Group cohesion creates safety and gives individual members the security and the self-confidence that goes along with belonging.

Friendships during the early teenage years wax and wane, and from one end of the school year to the next there will be shifts and realignments in friend groups. It is rare for a friendship group to remain entirely intact over a six-month period. These shifting friendships can be very stressful for teenagers and some teenagers end up feeling excluded and lonely. By late adolescence the internal tensions in peer groups settle. The friend group becomes a second family and a source of huge emotional support.

Reduce Relationship Stress Through Creating Space

One reason why relationships are stressful is that everybody shows up with baggage from their previous relationships. Imagine queuing to get on a budget flight in high season. Everybody rocks up for the flight with an over-stuffed wheelie suitcase of previous hurts, feelings of being not quite good enough and fears of rejection. This baggage keeps bumping up against the other passengers' over-stuffed suitcases. Inevitably there are misunderstandings, bruised feelings and the occasional stand-up row.

Sometimes we take relationship stress too personally. We feel like the other person is banging up against us intentionally, and of course sometimes they are. We have all seen that passenger who is willing to take your eye out to get their luggage in the overhead locker before you do. But most of the time the bumps are accidental. The person who banged into you is just harried and worried and their mind is elsewhere.

One of the ways of reducing relationship stress is to try to be a little more 'spacious' when dealing with other people. Instead of being crammed on a budget flight, imagine what it is like when everybody can lay out flat in the first-class cabin. No bumping, no rushing, no worries about where you are going to stash your suitcase or whether or not there is going to be any chicken and stuffing sandwiches left by the time the food trolley reaches you.

Being spacious in a relationship means allowing that other people sometimes do or say things that hurt and upset you without that being their intention. It is just that their wheelie suitcase bumped up against you. They didn't purposively wheel it into you. When somebody accidentally bumps into us we can choose to be gracious and say 'no bother', or we can get all up in their face and shout at them for being rude and ignorant.

The next exercise helps you create some space in a relationship that is stressed. It is called *Loving Eyes*. You can get a sense of what having loving eyes feels like by thinking of something that always makes you smile, such as puppies, kittens or babies. Then go on YouTube and find some cute videos. Notice when you smile how the muscles around your eyes soften and a good feeling spreads to the rest of your body. This is the kind of feeling you want to generate while you are doing *Loving Eyes*.

You can practise this when you are on your own and you can use it in real time when you feel fed up with someone, and they are really testing your patience. Instead of raising your eyes to heaven, try some loving eyes instead. How we look at people affects the way they look at us. When we smile other people smile back, but when we look at people with hostility they react defensively.

Loving Eyes

- Place your hands on your heart, one on top of the other. Gently and slowly focus on exhaling, take a pause, and then allow your next inward breath to fill and expand your heart and chest. Repeat this for another two outward breaths, each time trying to increase the length of your outward breath a little.
- Let your breathing return to normal.
- Bring to mind the face of a person with whom there is relationship stress. It could be a friend, a partner, a parent or a sibling.
- Imagine looking at this person through loving eyes. Bring awareness to your eyes and notice any tension. Invite a smile into your eyes and allow the muscles around your eyes to soften.
- Bring your attention to your thoughts and feelings.
  - Notice any stories that come to mind.
  - Notice how you feel about smiling at this person.
  - Maybe it feels like a relief to be smiling or maybe you don't want to smile. That's okay, just notice what is there.
- Ask yourself 'What would it be like if our relationship could be a little more spacious right now?' Imagine that first-class cabin!

Careful Communication Reduces Relationship Stress

The key to all relationships is communication. Most of the stress in relationships comes from miscommunication. Good communication is made up of listening and speaking carefully. 'Carefully' has two meanings. The first is doing something while showing thought and attention. The second is making sure to avoid danger or harm. Mindfulness helps you communicate carefully by showing thought and attention in the way you listen to the other person, and taking the time to avoid saying anything harmful and unnecessary when you speak.

Listening carefully involves paying attention to what the other person is saying without doing any of the following:

- Jumping to conclusions
- Rehearsing in your mind what your response is going to be
- Making judgements
- Interrupting
- Giving advice about what the other person should do or say

Speaking carefully involves thinking about what you say. Imagine your friend forgot about your birthday and you feel upset. How would you talk to your friend about it? The mnemonic THINK provides a useful acronym for careful speech. Here is an explanation:

True	Is it true?
	Is what you are saying factually true? Don't exaggerate or inflame the situation by starting off with something like 'You never think about me'.
Helpful	Is it helpful?
	Make sure what you are saying will be helpful to the conversation. If you are dealing with a current situation it is usually not helpful to bring up issues from the past like 'Remember two years ago, when we were on holidays, and you left me stranded'.

I	Am I saying what I feel?
	Focus on using 'I' statements such as 'I feel' and 'I prefer'. Avoid saying things like 'you should' or 'I know you'. Rather than saying 'You are selfish and you need to learn to think about other people' go with 'I felt hurt that you forgot. It made me feel like I am not important to you'.
Necessary	Is it necessary?
	Does what you plan to say need to be said, or could you leave it unsaid? Stay focused on the situation in hand. There is no need to add in something like 'Did you know that my mother has never liked you. She warned me against you'.
Kind	Is it kind?
	Speak from a place of kindness where your intention is to ease relationship stress. At the same time, remember that sometimes it is necessary to point out problems in order to be kind.

The next exercise helps you to develop a careful approach to communication. It encourages you to put your attention on the other person instead of being caught up in your head. This ensures that the other person has the experience of being listened to. When people feel heard they are more receptive to the things we are trying to communicate.

Careful Communication

- Focus on the person to whom you are listening. Give them your complete attention. Here are some of the things you might focus on:

- Listen to the tone of their voice
- Notice their facial expressions
- Notice the energy in what they are saying. Is it fast, slow, flat, spiky, excited, noisy, quiet?
- Listen to the language they are using. Is the language dramatic or understated?

■ While you continue to listen and pay attention to the other person, start to notice what is happening inside you.
- What feelings come up in you as you listen?
- What thoughts distract you from listening?
- Are you willing to really hear the other person's perspective, or do you get caught up in making judgements and finding fault?
- Are you busy trying to get in and have your say?

■ Ask yourself what it would be like if you were a little more relaxed and open right now?

■ Wait until the other person is finished speaking before you speak. Use the THINK skills to help you decide what you are going to say.

Adult Taming

Teenagers want to be independent and think and speak for themselves. Parents and adults can find this difficult. It can take them quite a while to get used to the fact that the child they have known since birth is growing up and growing away. Parents feel anxious about teenagers' safety and their capacity to know their limits, and they feel rejected when teenagers want to spend more time with friends than with family. When a teenager looks at a parent as though they are the most embarrassing, most out of touch and most incredibly irritating person in the universe, most parents have a bad reaction.

By the way, the teenager may not be aware that they are giving their parents a look like that, but ask any parent and they will lament the way in which their once loving child now looks at them. I always ask teenagers to try and remember that once upon a time when they were a very little person their parents were the centre of their world, and at that time the sun, moon and stars shone from their parents' eyes. Being the centre of another human's universe is a very lovely feeling and it is something that parents find difficult to let go of when their children grow up and assert their independence.

Some parent–teenager conflict is an important rite of passage but for most teenagers keeping their parents on side can make life much easier. Sometimes when teenagers are dealing with their parents and trying to assert their independence, they can find it difficult to communicate in a way that is heard by their parents. This is not necessarily the teenager's fault – when communication issues arise between two people no one person is entirely to blame. Parents have their own over-stuffed wheelie suitcase, and often find themselves quite challenged when it comes to communicating with their teenagers. Indeed the parent's inner teenager frequently surfaces and gets into a battle with their teenage son or daughter.

The next exercise provides a framework for mindful negotiations. This framework can help you overcome communication difficulties with the adults in your life. Read through the framework carefully. Before you attempt a negotiation make some short notes about what you want to say. If you are feeling particularly angry or frustrated with the adult spend two to three minutes doing *Loving Eyes* before you start the negotiation. This should take some of the heat out of your feelings and help you find a way to strike a positive tone. Directly before you sit down to have the conversation hit the pause button with the *Mindful STOP* to calm any anxiety or strong feelings. This helps create some space so the conversation gets off to a good start.

Mindful Negotiations Framework

- **Clear:** Be clear about the topic you want to discuss. Stick to one topic per negotiation. This could be negotiating a later curfew, going to a concert on a school night, or getting permission for an overnight trip with friends.

- **Choose your time:** Timing is key in a good negotiation. Don't try to have a conversation when you or the other person are distracted, hungry, busy or distressed. Find a time that suits you both, when you both can give the conversation your full attention. Here is a top tip: parenting books often suggest to parents that they talk to their children in the car; this works equally well for teenagers who want to engage with their parents!

- **Focus:** Focus on the topic, and don't let yourself get sidetracked. Remember the *Clouds Go Sailing By* exercise, where every time you noticed yourself getting distracted you refocused on the clouds? In this conversation, every time you feel the conversation going off topic, respectfully bring it back to the topic you want to discuss.

- **Listen:** Be prepared to listen to what the other person says, and show that you have heard by explaining your understanding of what they have said. If you don't understand what they have said, or why they have said it, ask them to explain. Ask questions like 'I don't understand why you think I won't be safe at the concert so can you tell me what you are worried about?' or 'What did you mean when you said ...?' Remember to be respectful.

- **Flexible:** Try to be flexible. You may not get exactly what you hoped for, but you may get something close. Sometimes you have to give to get. Be ready to make a suitable offer in order to facilitate the negotiation. If you can't think of a good offer, consider asking the other person whether he or she has any ideas about how to resolve the situation. Remember that every time you reach a satisfactory compromise with this person, you are setting the stage for positive outcomes in future negotiations, and developing communication skills that will stand to you for your entire life.

- **Calm:** Do your best to remain calm throughout the discussion. If necessary, say to the other person that you are feeling frustrated and you want some breathing space to calm down. Use the *Mindful STOP* to maintain your calm. Walk away if you need to and schedule a later time to finish the conversation.
- **Aware:** Be aware of your tone of voice, facial expressions and gestures. The words you are saying may be reasonable, but if delivered in an angry, defensive or hostile tone of voice, the words won't come across as reasonable to the other person.

Cian's Story

Cian was dealing with depression that was expressed through anger and irritability, often directed at his family. In chapter six we saw how getting in touch with his values eased his relationship with his family, nonetheless he continued to struggle with his parents. He felt they interfered in his life too much, and, in comparison to many of his friends, he had to deal with stricter rules around his social life. Many of their rows were about what he was or was not allowed to do. He frequently broke their rules because he felt the rules were ridiculous. In turn this led to his parents clamping down tighter because in their eyes he could not be trusted. They believed that there had to be 'consequences' or else he would never learn.

Cian had been successfully using the *Mindful STOP* to deal with his emotions and he had developed good skills for managing his anger. I suggested he try using the mindful relationship skills to see if he could change the relationship with his parents. His first reaction to doing *Loving Eyes* was not positive:

> But I hate my Dad, I am so sick of consequences, consequences, consequences.

I reminded him that the practice was not intended to directly change how he felt. The goal is to just imagine looking at the other person with loving eyes and see what emerges. He agreed to try it as an experiment for a week. When he came back for the next session he told me that it had helped him to have some compassion for why his father was so strict. Cian told me that his uncle had been killed in an alcohol-related car accident in his early twenties. His father was very concerned about alcohol and wanted to ensure that Cian didn't drink. They insisted on picking him up early on nights out. This made Cian feel humiliated in front of his mates so he often chose to miss out on social occasions rather than deal with the embarrassment. It increased his feelings of loneliness and isolation, and, combined with the friction with his parents, was a significant contributor to his depression.

I asked Cian to keep in mind the over-stuffed wheelie suitcase his father was wheeling around, the grief and anger of losing a brother to an alcohol-related road death, and see if he could find a way to make some more space so there would be less friction between the two of them. At the same time I suggested he try negotiating for some more autonomy on his nights out. The football team were having a big night out to celebrate the end of the season, ending up with everybody staying over at a teammate's house, and Cian wanted to go.

Using the framework for *Mindful Negotiations Framework,* Cian reached an agreement with his father that his father would pick him up from town and give him a lift to his teammate's house. Previously Cian would have stormed off at this 'infringement' but the calmer, less volatile Cian decided he could turn it to his advantage, and tell his mates they could avoid expensive taxi fares, because his dad would pick them up.

When I finish with a client I always ask him or her what they found most helpful. Cian said that the work we did on his relationship with his dad helped the most. He found he could use what he learned in all of his relationships, and he found the metaphor of the over-stuffed wheelie suitcases particularly helpful when a relationship was stressful.

Summary

- We carry all our previous hurts, fears and sensitivities with us, and when these collide with the hurts, fears and sensitivities of others, the result is relationship stress.
- We can reduce relationship stress by changing how we communicate with and respond to others.
- Mindfulness helps us create a sense of spaciousness in our relationships, and this spaciousness reduces conflict and improves communication. Practising *Loving Eyes* regularly can help us to focus on the things we love about another person rather than the things that annoy us.

nine

Workout Extras

The mindfulness exercises described in chapters three to eight will help your teenager develop a core practice of mindfulness that supports mental fitness and emotional resilience in daily life. This section provides a variety of more targeted exercises tailored to particular areas that are common concerns in teenage life. It includes sections on:

- Social media and social networking
- Addictive and compulsive behaviours
- Exam and performance anxiety
- Sleepless nights
- Mood busting
- Coping when life gets tough

Social Media and Social Networking

Adults and teenagers speak different languages when it comes to social media and social networking. Teenagers separated from technology suffer from instant FOMO (fear of missing out), wanting to be connected and share constantly, while parents worry that their teenagers share too much. The language of social networking, a language of emojis and abbreviations, can seem foreign to parents and they often fear that their teenagers will forget how to communicate in more than one hundred and forty characters. Just as many people believed that telephone, radio and TV signalled the end of society when they were first invented, the same fears exist for the internet.

Attempts to turn back time in relation to social media and social networking are pointless. They hit a nexus of things that appeal to teenagers. The constant stimulation and real-time responses avert the dreaded boredom associated with the lower dopamine levels of the teenage brain. Likes on social media posts create an addictive dopamine spike with each increment. Social networking provides an amazing platform for communicating with peers. It directly answers teenagers' need for friendship beyond the family unit. It allows teenagers who are shy, have social anxiety, or have unusual or niche interests to remain engaged with their peers through group chats.

The social aspect of the internet has many positives though the negatives create concern for adults. Worries about grooming, bullying and exclusion are well founded and each parent must find their own way of addressing these issues with their teenagers. But on a more fundamental level parents today know less about their teenagers' lives than any previous generation of parents. Despite the constant ping of messages, it is difficult to tell with whom a teenager is communicating. As little as fifteen years ago, when I was parenting my first set of teenagers, their friends still called on that archaic technology now referred to as the 'landline'. I had a general sense of who they were hanging out with and what they were up to. With my second set of teenagers I only know who they are seeing by giving them a lift to a friend's house or when a gang of their friends gets ready for a night out at my house.

In my work with teenagers there are three areas that I typically address around how social media impacts their lives: communication and relating; distraction; addictive or compulsive usage.

Communication and Relating

Much of a teenager's self-esteem is based on where they fit in the social hierarchy. For kids who are struggling with low self-esteem the photoshopped, beautifully filtered and curated lives they see online increase their sense of loneliness and isolation. Certain kinds of bodies and looks get immediate approval through high numbers of likes. Within teenage circles there is a very narrow definition of what looks good and the pressure to fit in is strong. The popularity of health and fitness online with the mantra of 'strong is the new skinny' increases the pressure on teenagers to look good. I see more and more clients, both girls and boys, who are affected by orthorexia, an obsession with healthy eating and exercising, along with the more recognised eating disorders of anorexia and bulimia.

Status and prestige are instantly measurable online through the number of friends and the popularity of posts. Teenagers are very aware of where they fit in the hierarchies of cool and popular. Exclusion is played out through comments on posts. Somebody posts a group photo and a teenager with high status gets a stream of likes and comments, while the kids with lower statuses are dismissed through lack of mention. Teenagers are very sensitive to rejection, and a message that is not answered quickly or a photo that receives no comments or likes feels like life or death.

Everything online is instant and because it is instant it is for the most part instantly forgettable. It is not surprising that teenagers forget that everything posted online has four important characteristics, as described by Danah Boyd in her book on teenagers and social media, *It's Complicated*:

- **Persistent:** It is permanently stored in internet servers and so available to be recalled at a later stage any time in the future

- **Visible:** Depending on privacy settings it is potentially visible to a very wide audience
- **Spreadable:** It can be shared with a very wide audience instantly
- **Searchable:** Search engines make it is easy to find content about and written by anybody at any time

In the early nineties I worked in Silicon Valley and, along with using the internet for email and file sharing, we engaged socially through Usenet, the precursor to current social networking platforms. At that time Usenet was limited to the worldwide community of people who had regular access to the internet through their work. It was a community of nerds, geeks, anoraks and academics.

All the characteristics we see on social networking platforms today – the high sociability, the formation of groups of like-minded people with odd interests, and communication that ranged from enjoyable interactions through respectful debate to conflagration and trolling – were true of Usenet from the beginning. But at that time none of us knew how the internet would unfold and we had no idea that our posts would become searchable to the entire world twenty years later. My children can go online today and search the Usenet archives and see exactly what I posted, when I posted it, the machine I posted it from and the details of the people who were reading my posts over twenty five years ago. Much of the time we were ROTFL in good humour or arranging to meet up in RL, but of course at times we were flaming each other with derision. I might have posted differently if I had known that my children and my grandchildren could read those posts in the future.

With hindsight comes twenty-twenty vision, and so when I talk to teenagers I explain to them the characteristics of what they put up online, and suggest that they use the THINK communication skills (described in chapter eight) and take a *Mindful STOP* before hitting the send button. The exercise helps teenagers see how their engagement on social media is affecting them.

Mindful Social Media

- Gently and slowly focus on breathing out, take a pause, and then allow your next breath in to fill and expand your chest and tummy. Do this one more time, and then allow your breathing to return to normal.

- Read each update and before moving to the next update go through the following steps:

- Notice how the update effects you. How does it make you feel? Perhaps you feel excited, tense, nervous, happy, loved, jittery, angry, excluded, jealous, unsure or anxious.

- Notice if you want to respond. Ask yourself the following questions:
  - Why do I want to respond?
  - What will I say?
  - Will what I plan on saying fit within the THINK communication skills?

- If you decide to respond take a *Mindful STOP* before hitting send. Make sure you are happy with what you are putting out into the world.

- **Questions to ask yourself when you are finished:**
  - Did reading theses updates make me feel good about myself?
  - Did my responses fit with my values?
  - Would I be okay with my parents seeing what I wrote?
  - Would I be okay with everybody at school seeing what I wrote?

- Would I be OK with my grandchildren reading what I wrote back to me in fifty years' time?

Distraction

Every alert on a phone, whether it is a beep, vibrating or flashing light, diverts a teenager's attention. But even when they put the phone away research shows that they continue to be distracted because they worry they are missing something important in a group chat, the latest viral YouTube video or that they haven't clocked up enough likes for their latest cover photo.

In his research on the impact of incoming texts on concentration, Larry Rosen found that students who were able to wait a couple of minutes before responding to a text did much better than those that responded immediately (Rosen, 2013). For teenagers trying to study for important exams, increasing their capacity to manage the distraction of social media is vital.

This practice can be used any time and any place. The only requirement is to have your phone close to you and visible, with all alerts turned on. It provides instant feedback on how distracted you are by social media, and as you practise over time it provides clear feedback on any improvements you make in your capacity to concentrate in the face of distraction.

Distraction Dimmer

- Gently and slowly focus on breathing out, take a pause, and then allow your next breath in to fill and expand your chest and tummy. Do this one more time, and then allow your breathing to return to normal.
- Count each inhale. Every time you notice that you have gotten distracted and have stopped counting, go back to one and start again.

- Notice what happens each time you see or hear an alert:
  - Do you immediately want to see what it is about?
  - What is it like to wait?
  - Can you keep counting as the alerts come in?
  - How many breaths do you manage to count before you get so distracted that you have to start counting from one again?

Addictive and Compulsive Behaviours

In chapter two we looked at how the reward system of the teenage brain can lead teenagers to become dependent on a variety of things such as alcohol, junk food, exercise, computer games and social media to manage their emotions and feed their dopamine-hungry reward system.

Dependencies quickly become habit forming, and it takes a twofold approach to break the habits. Firstly, the emotion-regulation skills needed to manage difficult and overwhelming feelings must be put in place. Chapters three to seven focus on developing these skills, which, once in place, will provide protection against the development of new dependencies. Unfortunately the development of emotion-regulation skills is rarely enough to break existing dependencies.

Mindfulness has been successfully used in addiction treatment programmes. G. Alan Marlatt developed the concept of urge surfing as part of a programme of relapse prevention (Marlatt, 1999). He noted that urges for substances rarely last very long, certainly no longer than thirty minutes, but often much shorter than that. Urges are like ocean waves that start small, grow in size, until they crest and break on the shore. Then they break up and recede back into the ocean.

One analogy involves thinking about an urge as a stray cat demanding to be fed. In the beginning you feel sorry for the cat and give it a saucer of milk. You feel good about being kind. But soon all the stray cats in the area realise you are an easy touch and come caterwauling for food and attention and scrapping outside your bedroom window. If you don't feed the first cat it will find food elsewhere. Similarly, if we don't feed our cravings, over time they become less demanding.

You can use the *Urge Surfing* exercise anytime you notice yourself having an urge or craving. If you are in the middle of dealing with an addictive or compulsive behaviour it is worth setting aside regular time to practise using this technique.

Urge Surfing

- Gently and slowly focus on breathing out, take a pause, and then allow your next breath in to fill and expand your chest and tummy. Do this one more time, and then allow your breathing to return to normal.

- Where do you feel the urge in your body? Often people feel urges in their stomach or their mouth. You might feel it in more than one place.

- Start with the body part where the urge feels most intense. Notice the sensations.

  • What does it feel like? Perhaps there are feelings of pressure, warmth, coolness, tingling or tightness.

  • How much space do these sensations take up in your body?

  • If the sensations had a colour, what colour would that be?

- Bring your attention back to your breath. Notice your breath for the next minute.

- Turn your attention away from your breathing and bring it back to the part(s) of the body where you noticed the urge. Imagine the sensations associated with the urge are like a wave and you are using your breath to help surf that wave. Sometimes it helps to describe the sensations in your head. Keep doing this until you notice the urge start to subside.

Exam and Performance Anxiety

Teenagers are under huge pressure to perform well in all areas of their lives. The pressure is enormous and at no time greater than during preparation for the Leaving Certificate or A Level. Teenagers believe that the whole of their future lives rest on how well they do in a two-hour exam that tests two years of study and learning. A little bit of stress is helpful and increases concentration and alertness; however, too much anxiety causes brain freeze and a desperate feeling of wasting precious minutes while waiting for the anxiety to subside.

Do the next exercise as you sit in the examination hall waiting for the papers to be passed to ensure that your brain is primed to get started as soon as you open the exam paper. Practise this exercise during class tests so that it becomes second nature at the outset of every exam, you do. If you find yourself getting a brain freeze during the exam, do the exercise again and remember that, even though it feels like hours, in reality the brain freeze will be measured in seconds if you consciously and mindfully calm your anxiety.

This exercise can be used in any situation that creates anxiety: exams; sporting competitions; public speaking; social occasions.

Ready – Get Set – Exam

- Gently and slowly focus on breathing out, take a pause, and then allow your next breath in to fill and expand your chest and tummy. Do this one more time, and then allow your breathing to return to normal.
- Press your feet into the floor, rolling them from the heel to the toes and back again a couple of times.
- Bring your attention to the sensation of the chair you are sitting on supporting your legs and your back.

- Look around the room and notice five things. For each thing describe it in your head. For example, 'There is a white clock on the wall. The wall is painted grey. The person in front of me has a red pencil case. The examiner is wearing a blue shirt.'

Sleepless Nights

Sleep is vital to physical and emotional health. Teenagers need nine to ten hours sleep per night but most teenagers get closer to seven hours, and some even less. Lack of sleep affects every area of your life. You can't concentrate. Your blood sugar plummets during the day and you end up reaching for sugary snacks. You become irritable. You fight with your friends and your family. Your immune function reduces and you become prone to infections. Over a period of time, lack of sleep affects your overall mood and can trigger depression. Depression then impacts sleep, creating a vicious cycle that makes daily life very challenging.

There are a number of reasons why sleep can be difficult for teenagers. Their body clock is set on a later sleep cycle than adults and so they don't feel sleepy at 11 p.m., the time they would need to be asleep to get a regular eight hours of sleep and make it to school on time. The teenager's constant quest for stimulation due to low dopamine levels leads to a busy mind, making it difficult to fall asleep.

Much of the stimulation comes from phones, computers and TV. The glow from these electronic devices prevents the release of melatonin, a hormone that helps the body get ready for sleep. Teenagers are more susceptible than adults to the impacts of light, while exposure impacts the length of time they sleep and the quality of sleep they get.

Sleep experts recommend turning screens off at least one hour before sleep time, but unfortunately most teenagers reward themselves with screen time of one kind or another after an evening of study. Turning down screen brightness and using filters that shift the colour of light from blue to reds and yellows can help. There are apps available that will do this automatically for phones, tablets and laptops.

If you find that you are not getting enough good quality, regular sleep, here are a number of things that you can do to improve your chances of refreshing sleep:

- Keep your bedroom dark
- Have a regular bedtime and a regular wake time
- Turn off screens one hour before bed
- Don't drink caffeine-based drinks after 3 p.m. In particular watch out for 'energising' drinks that have high caffeine content
- Get twenty to thirty minutes exercise during the day, even if that is just walking to and from school
- Use the *Sleepytime Bodyscan* exercise when you go to bed to help calm the body and mind in readiness for sleep

Sleepytime Bodyscan

- Lie on your back. Gently and slowly focus on breathing out, take a pause, and then allow your next breath in to fill and expand your chest and tummy. Do this one more time, and then allow your breathing to return to normal.
- Imagine putting all your worries and concerns into a box. Close the lid of the box and put in place an intention to leave the worries in the box till the following morning.
- Feel the bed underneath you. Feel how it supports the weight of your body.
- Bring your attention to your head. As you exhale, feel the weight of your head sinking into the pillow.
- Bring your attention to your shoulders. As you exhale feel your shoulders and upper back sink into the bed.

- Bring your attention to your arms and hands. As you exhale, feel your arms and hands get heavy, and sink into the bed.
- Bring your attention to your back. As you exhale, feel your back get heavy, sink into the bed.
- Bring your attention to your buttocks. As you exhale, feel your buttocks get heavy and sink into the bed.
- Bring your attention to your thighs. As you exhale, feel your thighs get heavy and sink into the bed.
- Bring your attention to your calves. As you exhale, feel your calves get heavy and sink into the bed.
- Bring your attention to your heels and feet. As you exhale, feel your heels and feet get heavy and sink into the bed.
- Any time you notice yourself getting hooked by your thoughts, gently let them go and bring your attention back to your body, noticing the contact between your body and the bed.
- If you notice any tension in your body, place your attention on the tension for a couple of breaths, imagining that as you breathe in the tension softens, and as you breathe out the tension releases.
- When you reach your feet start scanning from your head once more.
- When you feel sleepy turn over into your favourite sleeping position and let your breathing slow down as you drift into sleep.

Mood Busting

Teenagers don't have a very good sense of time, and when they feel down, it can seem like those feelings might never end. In reality, they will be high on the joys of life twenty minutes later. One of the things I encourage teenagers to do is to learn that they can alter their moods in entirely legal and totally safe ways. Here are some ways to consciously improve a low mood:

- Watch an episode of your favourite sitcom
- Look for funny videos online
- Chat to a friend
- Go for a run
- Organise a social event
- Play with the family pet
- Make a cake and share it with people you like
- Borrow your neighbour's dog and take it for a walk

This mindfulness exercise creates an instant feel-good factor. Before you start, choose a happy memory, something uncomplicated that automatically brings a smile to your face. The *Mood Buster* only takes one minute to do, and you should make it a regular part of your daily mindfulness exercise routine.

Mood Buster

- Gently and slowly focus on breathing out, take a pause, and then allow your next breath in to fill and expand your chest and tummy. Do this one more time, and then allow your breathing to return to normal.
- Focus on your chest and heart. Imagine your breath is flowing in and out of your heart, and that on each inhale it feels as though your heart is expanding a little.
- Bring your happy memory to mind. Make it vivid and bright as though it is happening right now.
- Imagine breathing this happy memory into your heart. Notice how your heart feels right now.
- Have the sense of smiling inwardly at yourself and thank yourself for taking the time to do this practice.

Coping When Life Gets Tough

During the teenage years there will be many times that a teenager feels overwhelmed by life circumstances such as:

- Relationship break-ups
- Bereavement
- Parental separation and divorce
- Changes in financial circumstances
- Loss of friendships
- Anxiety about exams and the future
- Existential anxiety and identity concerns

The next mindfulness exercise provides a framework for dealing with the difficult feelings that complex emotional situations trigger. It is not a panacea or a cure, rather an approach for self-soothing when times are tough. The acronym RAIN provides an easy-to-remember mnemonic:

- Recognise what is going on
- Allow the experience to be there, just as it is
- Investigate the experience with friendly curiosity
- Nourish the self with kindness and care

RAIN

- Gently and slowly focus on breathing out, take a pause, and then allow your next breath in to fill and expand your chest and tummy. Do this one more time, and then allow your breathing to return to normal.

- **Recognise**
  The first step is just to recognise that you are all caught up in feelings. Just breathe, focusing on your outward breath. Recognise that there are a lot of feelings swirling around. Saying a phrase like 'I feel so much distress right now' can be enough to start the process of noticing the different feelings. Take a breath or two to pause and acknowledge that right now things are really tough.

- **Allow**
  The next step is about making a choice to stand your ground instead of resisting the feelings, running away or distracting yourself. Instead of heading the feelings off using any of your usual coping strategies, agree to go through these feelings right now as they come up. Just allow the feelings to be there. There is no suggestion that you have to like the feelings, or believe that the situation in which you find yourself is okay or fair. Right now you are just creating space for the feelings. In a way it is like saying, 'Yes this totally sucks but nonetheless I agree to have these feelings'. Often this brings an immediate sense of the feelings softening and shifting, reminding you that the feelings will pass.

- **Investigate**
  In this step it is time to put on your Sherlock Holmes hat and investigate what is going on. Start with what is happening inside your body. See what kind of sensations you are experiencing. This is not an exhaustive list of possibilities but it is a good start:

  - How is your breath? Shallow, fast, ragged, difficult, soft, slow.

  - How is your temperature? Are some parts of your body hot and other parts of your body cold?

- Is your head throbbing?
- Is your chest tight?
- How fast or slow is your heartbeat?

  After you have investigated the sensations take some time to investigate the wider circumstances that might be influencing the feelings. How was my mood when this situation happened? Had I eaten enough? Did I get enough sleep last night? Did this remind me of something similar from the past that might lead me to feel overwhelmed by feelings in the present?

- **Nourish**
  Notice that something in you feels this way, but something in you can notice having the feeling. You might say to yourself 'I am more than these feelings'. Move from being caught up in the feelings to being in observer mode. Instead of noticing that *you* are jealous/angry/sad, notice that *something in you feels* jealous/angry/sad. Offer that *something* peace, love, kindness and the willingness to be alongside. Remind yourself that these feelings will pass.

- **Questions to ask yourself when you are finished:**
  - How was my mood when this situation happened?
  - Had I eaten enough?
  - Did I get enough sleep last night?
  - Are there simple things I could do in my life right now to take better care of myself?

Mental Health for Teenagers

The techniques described in this book build mental fitness and emotional resilience through encouraging the development of emotion regulation. Nonetheless, a teenager who is currently dealing with a mental health issue needs more directed help. Research shows that about one in five adolescents is at risk of developing a mental health issue. About 75 per cent of all mental health problems first emerge between the ages of fifteen to twenty-five (Dooley, 2012). In Ireland the mortality rate from suicide in that age group is the fourth highest in the EU, rising to third highest among young men aged between fifteen and nineteen. Unfortunately, only a small minority of these teenagers get professional help.

Sometimes people find it difficult to distinguish between normal teenage angst and behaviours that indicate that the teenager may require professional support. First of all, trust your intuition. If you think a teenager's behaviour is a matter for concern, it probably is. The most common mistake I see is that adults believe that the teenager is just going through a phase. Catching mental health problems early leads to better outcomes but sometimes people are concerned that the teenager will be labelled for life. Check your teenager's behaviour against the descriptions in the following table to help you determine if there might be a mental health concern, but remember that any mention of suicidal thoughts or any suggestion that the teenager sees or hears things that others do not indicates that there is need for immediate assessment.

When it comes to teenage mental health it is best to err on the side of caution. Simple interventions at an early stage can prevent the development of more serious problems. If you are an adult living with a teenager who has a mental health issue, make sure to get help for yourself. Remember the advice on airplanes: put on your own oxygen mask before helping your child with theirs.

Normal Teenage Behaviour	Behaviour that might mean your teenager is struggling with a mental health issue
Wanting to spend more time with friends and less time with family	Withdrawing from friendships and from family relationships
Occasional lateness for school due to difficulty getting up in the morning	Consistent complaints of exhaustion and low energy causing lateness for school
Occasional missed days from school	Strong resistance to attending school or consistent absenteeism
Changes in appetite (either eating more or less) that last no longer than a couple of weeks	Sudden changes in appetite that continue for more than a couple of weeks accompanied by quick fluctuations in weight
Bouts of sadness and anxiety related to life events such as break-ups or disagreements with friends	Sadness and anxiety that lasts longer than two weeks and does not diminish in intensity
Some minor risk-taking or experimentation with alcohol, drugs, sex	Extreme and dangerous risky behaviour or thrill-seeking that does not decrease in face of adult concern
Telling occasional lies, in particular lies that concern pushing boundaries in social life, e.g. saying they are studying in a friend's house when in fact they are going out socially with their mates	Consistent lying, frequent aggression, conduct problems or lashing out verbally that causes concern at school or at home

Occasional concerns about physical appearance and the need to fit in	Sudden and significant changes in eating and exercising behaviours. Remember that boys are at risk of eating disorders as well as girls
Occasional emotional outbursts, getting tearful over minor episodes, and general grumpiness	Consistent irritation and angry outbursts that are accompanied by withdrawal from relationships. Remember that teenage anxiety and depression is expressed differently and does not present in the same way as adult depression and anxiety
Occasional lack of sleep, causing the teenager to spend a good part of the weekend catching up on sleep	Consistent difficulties with sleep accompanied by low energy and lack of motivation
Occasional concerns related to personal hygiene and appearance	Excessive neglect of personal hygiene and appearance

Often teenagers turn to their peers for help first. This puts a significant burden on their friends, who do their best to help, but are ill-equipped to offer meaningful support to a teenager dealing with a mental health issue. When I work with teenagers who have mental health issues I usually discover that they disclosed these issues to a friend long before the adults in their lives realised there was a problem.

Talk to the teenagers in your life about what to do if a friend is having difficulties, and explain to them the warning signs that indicate that professional help should be sought.

This means that they can encourage their friends to seek help and protects them from becoming overburdened by their friends' problems.

If you are concerned about a teenager's mental health, then counselling and psychotherapy are a good place to start. Ask your GP for referrals to a psychotherapist that works specifically with adolescents. When choosing a psychotherapist check the following:

- The professional is fully trained and accredited by a professional body such as ICP, PSI or IACP.
- The professional provides clear information about his or her qualifications, how he or she works, fees, confidentiality, the length of the sessions and the duration of the work.
- You feel confident in the professional after you have spoken to him or her. Trust your own intuition more than the letters that come after his or her name.
- Your teenager feels a connection with the professional and feels comfortable talking to him or her. Research consistently shows that the success of psychotherapy depends more on how the client views the relationship than any other single factor.
- Don't worry too much about what approach the professional uses. Research shows that in the final analysis most approaches work well when used by a competent and well-trained professional. The most important thing is that the approach used makes sense to the individual seeking treatment.

In addition to getting professional help there are many things you can do at home to support your teenager.

- **Make one-on-one time a priority:** Set aside time most days to spend with the teenager face-to-face. This can be spent chatting, doing chores together, watching a box set, or taking the dog for a walk. The goal is not to talk to the teenager about their problems, rather to offer them a steady and warm sense of connection. The simple act of connecting plays a huge role in reducing distress and promoting good mental health.

- **Reduce social isolation:** Do what you can to keep your teenager connected to peers. Make it easy for them to see their friends.

- **Get your teenager involved:** Make it easy for your teenager to engage in a variety of activities. It is really beneficial for a teenager to have more than one sphere of involvement, so that they have friends from different social circles. If a teenager is having difficulty with peers in school, it can be very supportive for them to have peers they enjoy spending time with at activities not related to school, such as sports, drama, scouts or music.

- **Encourage exercise:** Get your teenager moving. Exercise has been shown to help many mental health issues. It doesn't have to be formal exercise – cycling to school, walking the dog, skateboarding, trailing around the park with mates – anything as long as it involves moving. Model healthy approaches to exercise in your own life.

- **Provide nutritious meals:** Make sure your teenager is getting healthy, balanced meals that include protein, dairy, healthy carbohydrates, vegetables and fruit. Don't keep a lot of starchy or sweet snacks in the house and encourage them to limit their consumption of sweets, chocolate, sugary and stimulating drinks (including fruit juice).

- **Limit alcohol in the home:** Remember that alcohol acts as a depressant, and is commonly implicated in teenage suicide. Too often in Ireland we complain about the amount that teenagers drink, but we don't reflect on our own habits with regard to alcohol. Model a healthy relationship with alcohol in your family and in your home, and if your teenager is dealing with a mental health issue, ensure that they don't have easy access to alcohol at home, or through older siblings and friends.

- **Encourage good sleep:** Teens need more sleep than adults, up to nine or ten hours a night. Because their circadian rhythms are set differently to adults' they tend to be nocturnal animals. Help teenagers to understand the negative impacts that lack of sleep has on their mental health and talk to them about ways of getting more sleep. You will find further ideas about encouraging good sleep in the section on sleepless nights in this chapter.

- **Encourage healthy independence:** Developing healthy separation and independence from parents is the single most important thing that a teenager needs to do for lasting mental fitness and emotional resilience in adult life. Too often I see teenagers whose quests for independence have been thwarted; or the opposite, they have been given too much independence with a lack of appropriate boundaries and limits at too early an age. Both ends of the dependence–independence spectrum contribute in different ways to mental health issues.

bibliogaphy

One: Start Where You Are

Baird, B., Smallwood, J., Mrazek, M.D., Kam, J.W.Y., Franklin, M.S. and Schooler, J.W., 'Inspired by Distraction: Mind Wandering Facilitates Creative Incubation', *Psychological Science*, Vol. 23, No. 10 (2012), pp. 1117–22. doi. org/10.1177/0956797612446024

Black, D.S. and Slavich, G.M. 'Mindfulness meditation and the immune system: a systematic review of randomized controlled trials', *Annals of the New York Academy of Sciences*, Vol. 1373, No. 1 (2016), pp. 13–24. doi.org/10.1111/nyas.12998

Children's Society, *The Good Childhood Inquiry: Health Research Evidence*, London: Children's Society, 2008.

Jensen, F.E., *The Teenage Brain*, London: Harper Thorsons, 2015.

Tang, Y.-Y., Ma, Y., Wang, J., Fan, Y., Feng, S., Lu, Q., ... Posner, M.I., 'Short-term meditation training improves attention and self-regulation', *Proceedings of the National Academy of Sciences*, Vol. 104, No. 43 (2007), pp. 17152–6. doi. org/10.1073/pnas.0707678104

Weare, K., 'Evidence for the impact of mindfulness on children and young people', 2012, nora-school.org/admin-forms/mindfulness-studies.pdf

WHO, *Caring for Children and Adolescents with Mental Disorders: Setting WHO Directions*, Geneva: World Health Organization, 2003. who.int/mental_health/media/en/785.pdf

Zeidan, F., Martucci, K.T., Kraft, R.A., McHaffie, J.G. and Coghill, R.C., 'Neural correlates of mindfulness meditation-related anxiety relief', *Social Cognitive and Affective Neuroscience*, Vol. 9, No. 6 (2014), pp. 751–9. doi.org/10.1093/scan/nst041

Two: Pack Up Your Kitbag

Anderson, J.E., 'Brain Development in Adolescents: New Research – Implications for Physicians and Parents in Regard to Medical Decision Making', *Issues in Law & Medicine*, Vol. 30, No. 2 (2015), pp. 193–6.

Decety, J. and Cacioppo, J.T. (eds), *The Oxford Handbook of Social Neuroscience*, New York; Oxford: Oxford University Press, 2011.

Guyer, A.E., Monk, C.S., McClure-Tone, E.B., Nelson, E.E., Roberson-Nay, R., Adler, A.D., ... Ernst, M., 'A Developmental Examination of Amygdala Response to Facial Expressions', *Journal of Cognitive Neuroscience*, Vol. 20, No. 9 (2008), pp. 1565–82. doi.org/10.1162/jocn.2008.20114

Lieberman, M.D., Eisenberger, N.I., Crockett, M.J., Tom, S.M., Pfeifer, J.H. and Way, B.M., 'Putting feelings into words: affect labeling disrupts amygdala activity in response to affective stimuli', *Psychological Science*, Vol. 18, No. 5 (2007), pp. 421–8. doi.org/10.1111/j.1467-9280.2007.01916.x

Maguire, E.A., Woollett, K. and Spiers, H.J., 'London taxi drivers and bus drivers: A structural MRI and neuropsychological analysis', *Hippocampus*, Vol. 16, No. 12 (2006), pp. 1091–101. doi.org/10.1002/hipo.20233

Reyna, V.F., Estrada, S.M., DeMarinis, J.A., Myers, R.M., Stanisz, J.M. and Mills, B.A., 'Neurobiological and memory models of risky decision making in adolescents versus young adults', *Journal of Experimental Psychology: Learning, Memory, and Cognition*, Vol. 37, No. 5 (2011), pp. 1125–42. doi.org/10.1037/a0023943

Reyna, V.F. and Farley, F., 'Risk and Rationality in Adolescent Decision Making: Implications for Theory, Practice, and Public Policy', *Psychological Science in the Public Interest: A Journal of the American Psychological Society*, Vol. 7, No. 1 (2006), pp. 1–44. doi.org/10.1111/j.1529-1006.2006.00026.x

Steinberg, L., 'Risk Taking in Adolescence: What Changes, and Why?', *Annals of the New York Academy of Sciences*, Vol. 1021, No. 1 (2004), pp. 51–8. doi.org/10.1196/annals.1308.005

Steinberg, L., 'A social neuroscience perspective on adolescent risk-taking', *Developmental Review*, Vol. 28, No. 1 (2008), pp. 78–106. doi.org/10.1016/j.dr.2007.08.002

Bibliography

Three: Ride the Emotional Roller Coaster

Jack, R.E., Garrod, O.G.B. and Schyns, P.G., 'Dynamic Facial Expressions of Emotion Transmit an Evolving Hierarchy of Signals Over Time', *Current Biology*, Vol. 24, No. 2 (2014), pp. 187–92. doi.org/10.1016/j.cub.2013.11.064

Taylor, J.B., *My Stroke of Insight*, London: Hachette UK, 2009.

Six: Value Finding and Strength Spotting

Csikszentmihalyi, M., *Flow: The Psychology of Happiness: The Classic Work on How to Achieve Happiness* (new edn), London: Rider, 2002.

Jach, H.K., Sun, J., Loton, D., Chin, T.-C. and Waters, L.E., 'Strengths and Subjective Wellbeing in Adolescence: Strength-Based Parenting and the Moderating Effect of Mindset', *Journal of Happiness Studies*, pp. 1–20. doi.org/10.1007/s10902-016-9841-y

Peterson, C., Ruch, W., Beermann, U., Park, N. and Seligman, M.E., 'Strengths of character, orientations to happiness, and life satisfaction', *The Journal of Positive Psychology*, Vol. 2, No. 3 (2007), pp. 149–56.

Plumb, J.C., Stewart, I., Dahl, J. and Lundgren, T., 'In Search of Meaning: Values in Modern Clinical Behavior Analysis', *The Behavior Analyst*, Vol. 32, No. 1 (2009), pp. 85–103.

Proctor, C., Maltby, J. and Linley, P.A., 'Strengths use as a predictor of well-being and health-related quality of life', *Journal of Happiness Studies*, Vol. 12, No. 1 (2011), pp. 153–69.

Proctor, C., Tsukayama, E., Wood, A.M., Maltby, J., Eades, J.F. and Linley, P.A., 'Strengths gym: The impact of a character strengths-based intervention on the life satisfaction and wellbeing of adolescents', *The Journal of Positive Psychology*, Vol. 6, No. 5 (2011), pp. 377–88.

Wood, A.M., Linley, P.A., Maltby, J., Kashdan, T.B. and Hurling, R., 'Using personal and psychological strengths leads to increases in well-being over time: A longitudinal study and the development of the strengths use questionnaire', *Personality and Individual Differences*, Vol. 50, No. 1 (2011), pp. 15–19.

137

Seven: Taking Care of Number One

Crocker, J. and Park, L.E., 'The Costly Pursuit of Self-Esteem', *Psychological Bulletin*, Vol. 130, No. 3 (2004), pp. 392–414. doi.org/10.1037/0033-2909.130.3.392

Neff, K.D., 'Self-compassion, self-esteem, and well-being', *Social and Personality Psychology Compass*, Vol. 5, No. 1 (2011), pp. 1–12.

Neff, K.D., Hsieh, Y.-P. and Dejitterat, K., 'Self-compassion, achievement goals, and coping with academic failure', *Self and Identity*, Vol. 4, No. 3 (2005), pp. 263–87.

Neff, K.D. and McGehee, P., 'Self-compassion and psychological resilience among adolescents and young adults', *Self and Identity*, Vol. 9, No. 3 (2010), pp. 225–40.

Neff, K.D. and Vonk, R., 'Self-compassion versus global self-esteem: Two different ways of relating to oneself', Journal of Personality, Vol. 77, No. 1 (2009), pp. 23–50.

Parker-Pope, T., 'Go Easy on Yourself, a New Wave of Research Urges', *The New York Times*, 28 February 2011. well.blogs.nytimes.com/2011/02/28/go-easy-on-yourself-a-new-wave-of-research-urges/

Eight: Navigate Relationships Mindfully

James, W., *The Principles of Psychology*, New York: Dover. 1890.

Manning, C., Waldman, M., Lindsey, W., Newberg, A. and Cotter-Lockard, D., 'Personal Inner Values – A Key to Effective Face-to-Face Business Communication', *Journal of Executive Education*, Vol. 11, No. 1 (2013). digitalcommons.kennesaw.edu/jee/vol11/iss1/3

Nine: Workout Extras

Boyd, D., *It's Complicated: The Social Lives of Networked Teens*, New Haven: Yale University Press, 2014.

Carrotte, E.R., Vella, A.M. and Lim, M.S., 'Predictors of "Liking" Three Types of Health and Fitness-Related Content on Social Media: A Cross-Sectional Study', *Journal of Medical Internet Research*, Vol. 17, No. 8 (2015). doi.org/10.2196/jmir.4803

Dooley, B.A. and Fitzgerald, A., *My World Survey: National Study of Youth Mental Health in Ireland* (Technical Report),

Dublin: Headstrong and UCD School of Psychology, 2012. researchrepository.ucd.ie/handle/10197/4286

Koven, N.S. and Abry, A.W., 'The clinical basis of orthorexia nervosa: emerging perspectives', *Neuropsychiatric Disease and Treatment*, Vol. 11, No. 385 (2015). doi.org/10.2147/NDT. S61665

Marlatt, G.A. and Kristeller, J.L., 'Mindfulness and Meditation', in William R. Miller, *Integrating Spirituality into Treatment: Resources for Practitioners*, Washington, DC: American Psychological Association, 1999, pp. 67–84. doi. org/10.1037/10327-004

Rosen, L.D., Carrier, L.M. and Cheever, N.A., 'Facebook and texting made me do it: Media-induced task-switching while studying', *Computers in Human Behavior*, Vol. 29, No. 3, pp. 948–58.

Mental Health for Teenagers

Cannon, M., Coughlan, H., Clarke, M., Harley, M. and Kelleher, I., 'The Mental Health of Young People in Ireland: A Report of the Psychiatric Epidemiology Research Across the Lifespan (PERL) Group', *Psychiatry Reports*, Royal College of Surgeons in Ireland, 2013. epubs.rcsi.ie/psychrep/1